COLLECTING =DEAD= RELATIVES

An Irreverent Romp Through the Field of Genealogy

By Laverne Galeener-Moore

Illustrated by Randy Calhoun

Genealogical Publishing Co., Inc.

Published by Genealogical Publishing Co., Inc.
Baltimore, Maryland

Second printing 1987
Third printing 1989
Fourth printing 1992
Fifth printing 1995

Published by arrangement with Gateway Press
Library of Congress Catalogue Card Number 86-83000
International Standard Book Number 0-8063-1181-9
Made in the United States of America

Dedicated to Two Live Relatives.....

Jeannine HUBBARD

for nagging me into writing it in the
first place

and

Melanie R. MOORE

who, even though handicapped by a love of good
books and the proper use of the English language,
put it all aside and bravely managed to wade
through the entire text with a red pencil and
a critical eye, pointing out the most flagrant
grammatical catastrophes, inexcusable
typos and other literary blunders
(most of which remain in the
book). (How's that for
a run-on sentence,
Melanie?)

Contrary to certain other books,
the characters described in this book
are based on real people

Contents

Backword*

Collecting dead relatives has fast become a more popular hobby than gathering rocks or butterflies. Once GENE-ALOGY strikes, an otherwise rational human being finds himself or herself in danger of hanging out in grave-yards, libraries, county courthouses and other far-from-stimulating locations until he or she is forcibly carted off to a more peaceful spot. So, before you take such a drastic plunge, or even if you are already hopelessly addicted, you may wish to peruse the following definitive study of the peculiar people, problems and pitfalls of this fascinating, laborious and expensive way to waste your time.

Five years ago I had a slipped disc and no interest in my ancestors. Then a fateful package arrived in the mail, sent from a New York stranger bearing the same last

---

* Usually this section in a book is called the "Foreword", but since everything in genealogy is always aimed in the other direction, the standard term didn't seem appropriate. For you spelling whizzes who smugly think you've caught an atrocious error in the spelling of "Backword", you haven't. It isn't even a word!

name as my husband (the thoroughly *common* name of MOORE), containing a bunch of loose papers and charts, all scribbled over with information about some MOOREs who lived a long time ago in Indiana or Kansas or somewhere back there and seemed to spend a lot of time dying, getting married and being born. Included in the packet was an urgent request that my husband add to this pile of meaningless flotsam (or so it appeared to me at the time). Now Alan, who has terrible handwriting and even worse spelling, but is a pretty cooperative fellow, sat down and drew up his own messy little disconnected family tree, with names, dates, locations and scraggly lines running every which-way, which he then presented to me for approval. I figured if the guy back in New York was lucky enough to have a close friend in the F.B.I. (decoding section), maybe he would be able to figure out the jumble of hieroglyphics Alan had come up with. With that thought, I promptly put the whole boring business out of mind, the better to get back to spending my own valuable time grousing about my aching insides.

Poor patient Alan, who by then had had a gullet-full of hearing complaints about my lumbar region, decided to try a diversion and began diplomatically to suggest that I start getting together my own family history (a ploy he has undoubtedly since come to regret many times over). So he nagged and cajoled, and persuaded our grown children to at least give the appearance of acting mildly interested, till I finally half-heartedly took the bait and agreed to visit the local LDS Library. Alan didn't realize for awhile just what a bomb he had set off! Now, five years, many missed or poorly prepared meals, and thousands of uncomfortable miles in a VW later, I must confess we are a lot poorer in the bankbook, but we certainly do know more than I ever cared to know about our ancestors.

Hey, you ask, how does one start? With a "how-to" book, of course. I bought a paperback version (frugality seemed important at the time because who in their right mind would waste much money on such a silly hobby?). The book offered the sage advice (totally ignored by me, as it later turned out) that a wise, would-be researcher should just pick out one surname and concentrate only on it, thereby avoiding getting more confused than usual. Since my mother's side, I reasoned, were all dead Hungarians or live domesticated descendants who weren't speaking to each other, I figured the only choice left to me for this monumental undertaking was my father's family. The first ancestor on his side that anyone had ever heard of was a Frenchman who spelled his name even funnier than the modern way, fought in the American Revolution right alongside LAFAYETTE (or so it was claimed), and later had something to do with flatboats on the Ohio and Mississippi Rivers. I reckoned he would be a snap. (The sad fact is that I'm still looking.)

The "how-to" book, continuing on its merry way dispensing valuable suggestions, directed the reader to assemble all the information he or she already had about his or her family and proceed from there. Well, that sounded reasonable. What I had as a start was my father's official, proper given name (and the alias he adopted because he hated his official, proper given name), my grandfather's full formal moniker (misspelled), my grandmother's maiden surname (accompanied by an absolutely incorrect birth-state, I later discovered), the names and addresses of four older first-cousins (mostly alive, I thought), and all the names of my aunts and uncles (altogether deceased). Another treasure-trove to which the book alluded, one which it claimed could be found in most families, were those endless old stories droned over and over and over by the more ancient kinfolk, usually just prior to Going to Their Reward, as it was delicately called, and to which no one hung around to listen if they could possibly help it. Now it looked like I would be forced to try to dredge up a passable recollection of those tiresome little gems which, according to the expert, took on momentous importance. As you can see, I was fast becoming infected and, if the truth be known, will probably never recover from the bite of the genealogy bug. So began the great adventure!

Today, surrounded by three file cabinets stuffed to near bursting with Xeroxed copies of prized death certificates, a vast assortment of official family criminal charges, titillating land transactions of the 1700s in which an inordinate amount of time was spent describing various species of trees, though Lord knows why, and faded pictures of people no one can identify, not to mention a floor-to-ceiling bookcase of expensive genealogy books with no mention of my family in them, I can probably pass myself off as an expert. To further support this claim to expertise, I've just finished putting all the stuff I could find into a book of my own, a 718-page one, which no one will probably ever read because it's way too thick, not very exciting, and all about a surname no one has ever heard of anyway. Since I had enough typewriter ribbon, paper and free time left over from my literary endeavor, and I've been taught not to waste things, I thought the world might be ready to hear every minute and fascinating detail in the daily life of an average dead relative collector. So here goes. . . .

"If you cannot get rid of the family skeleton, you may as well make it dance."

George Bernard Shaw

Committed
Researchers

The most successful genealogical researchers are those with reasonable vision and a good bladder, who don't suffer from motion sickness. If you are already into tri-focals, you can minimize this obstacle with the use of a strong magnifying glass, or two or three. If you are a person who is determined to make continual runs to the rest-room, you will lose your projector, to say nothing of your continuity. Perhaps if you forced yourself to refrain from drinking coffee (or anything else) before your trip to the library or archives and ate only cheese, you might rectify *this* particular problem. Also, scientific studies done on motion sickness suggest that, if you insist on planting yourself in a darkened room, turning a projector-crank continuously for five or six hours or longer, you might not expect to find yourself at top performance level if you then rush right out and attempt to drive your car in heavy traffic. In fact, you might even experience some difficulty in rushing right out. For those over eighty years of age (and many genealogists fall in this age range), the problems mentioned here would surely compound to give them a highly memorable time. All of us have had at least one unpleasant experience of sitting next to a nauseated projector-operator in a genealogical research center. One never knows whether to flip their light off, or what.

If you feel you are a good candidate to take a flying leap into the field of genealogy, and you are at least minimally in control of the problems detailed above, there are certain primary implements you will need. Pens and pencils are nice, because you will be doing a mountain of writing, and, unless you prefer some other medium, paper is handy. If you are a woman (or a man in San Francisco) who carries a big purse, it would be wise to give up the habit and take to wearing overalls or something with pockets, because many facilities force you to check your handbag at the door. If you are in excellent physical shape, with not even one extra pound of fat on your structure, especially in the area of the posterior, you might want to carry along a pillow, because you will learn only too soon that sitting on hard library chairs hour after hour can paralyze your parts.

Another novel idea to consider strongly is to convert one of your pockets into a portable pharmacy containing aspirins, antacid pills to alleviate gas and heartburn, and little things you can eat without getting caught at it. Taking sandwiches or a Big Mac into a dignified research institution is tacky and just not done. Librarians get irritated by peanut butter on the microfiche, so are on continual alert, especially close to the noon-hour, for patrons with unusually active jaw movements. The result is instant ejection and the loss of one's dignity. Sea-sick pills may also be a necessity if the round-and-around-and-around motion of the spinning films bothers you (see motion sickness, above). If you have to drive your own vehicle after a day at the archives, you might want to monitor your right hand, wrist and fingers from time to time and be prepared to terminate your daily handle-turning activities well before you lose the use of them. And Ben-Gay might help bring down the swelling of whatever swells up.

Unless you are rich enough to buy your own research facility, stone-deaf, or taken to regularly munching-out on garlic, you are almost always going to have to share your favorite center with numerous other searcher types. The gamut, unfortunately, generally runs through the following categories:

The "I'M FIRST". (This person is at the top of the list because it is the only way she would have it.) Why, I don't know, but this designation is mostly made up of the female variety, aged between 60 and 90, a harridan who never smiles and bears a striking resemblance to the late General PATTON. She troops in to the entrance foyer, always before opening-time, and immediately bulldozes her way through all patiently-waiting would-be researchers till she is absolutely first in line, belly-up to the barricade, which is the restraining barrier barring the public from stampeding into the research area before the exact time of 8:00 A.M. Perhaps she was an Olympic runner in the 1930s and/or still maintains a conditioning course, because she is always first downstairs, upstairs, or into the elevator, elbowing aside those even a quarter of her age. She invariably manages to get to a specific projector first, *"her"* projector, and one can only vaguely imagine what feathers will fly and what the fate will be of some poor, unknowing soul who might, by accident or miracle one day, beat her to that particular piece of equipment.

The "BRIEFCASE MAGNET". Can be either sex. Brings one *large,* or two or three or more, briefcase(s), a shopping bag or two, a huge purse, and a conglomeration of notebooks, charts, tablets, and every imaginable size

scrap of paper. May have to check some of this parapher-
nalia at the entrance of the building, but manages to keep
a death-grip on the remainder. At first glance, the hauled-
in accumulation would appear to represent 565 years of
constant research at the very least, but since the person
attached to this junk is usually less than 90 years of age,
he or she must take very fast notes. One suspects that the
day's supply of fresh transcriptions will just be dumped in
with the rest (one wonders if it will ever be looked at
again), for how anyone could possibly locate a specific
item, then and there, to compare with anything else more
recently found, is beyond comprehension, a puzzle only
answerable by the briefcase-toter (who would, I expect,
have to look up the answer in his or her files). Obviously,
the only container that this person seems incapable of stor-
ing information in is his or her head.

The "NOISEMAKER or NOISEMAKERS". Usually a
male-female team, or a female-female couple, but can be
three or more of whatever is currently popular, or one
single individual fast approaching senility, or already
arrived, who simply enjoys talking to himself or herself
out loud. The more years one indulges in this particular
hobby of genealogy, the more danger one faces of being
diagnosed as a member of this caste. You will constantly
be confronted by them in archives, libraries or anywhere
others are trying to study or do research in a reasonably
quiet atmosphere (I've even got one here at home). There
you are in a typical situation, turning the crank on the
trusty old projector, in deep concentration, trying to zero
in on the surname for which you are searching—GALE-
ENER, GALEENER, GALEENER—when suddenly a
strong audible comes through loud and clear and constant: "PENDERGAST, PENDERGAST, PENDER-
GAST." And guess what surname you jot down in your

notes? These caterwaulling citizens tend to think everyone in the room wants to hear a recitation of whatever it is they have located on their film, are trying to locate, or can't seem to locate. Some of the poor ninnies in this category, in their defense, may be hard-of-hearing and perhaps assume that everyone else is also. But one of these days I am going to initiate a violent act on one of them (or a bunch of them, for that matter) in order to insure peace and quiet in the research center.

The "BORE". Of course the fact is clear to all of us and not debatable (even though the illustrator of this book had the temerity to disagree with me) that men always outnumber women in this grouping, because it is widely known that they talk more about unimportant subjects than we females do and, once started, they are nearly impossible to shut off. Regarding those in the genealogy field, if one of them gets you cornered in the dark recesses of a projector room or, worse still, in between the library shelves, you will be subjected to the unspeakable indignities of hearing all about his hopelessly boring lineage, while you can bet that you won't even be allowed a minute to interject any of *your* brilliant reportage about your own far more fascinating predecessors. So remember, if a man accosts you in a research center wearing a wild-eyed, passionate look on his face, and starts to open his mouth, you just *know* what he's after and, unless he's asking directions to the men's room, you'd best beat a hasty, ladylike retreat.

The "LOCAL BLUEBLOOD". Can be related to the "BORE", above. This classification includes anyone who has proven, is nearly to the point of proving, or "has a strong feeling" that they are descended from royalty. We will broadly interpret royalty, in this instance, to refer not only to those folks who wore crowns and intermarried so much they sometimes produced idiots, but also to those early-day British trouble-makers and dissidents who, instead of protesting in the streets carrying placards, booked passage on the *Mayflower*, and to other pioneer extroverts and radicals who did things to get attention so that they would get their names in the history books. When a researcher today connects with any of the above, you can bet you will hear about it, endlessly. And a noticeable change comes over them. They start sitting by themselves at the head of the table in the research facility, as called for by their new exalted station in life, away from the *hoi polloi*. They may go so far as to attach a customized plastic Coat-of-Arms to their car's license plate or to their clipboard, lest you forget their status, or embroider a metallic-threaded crest on their muu-muu or tee-shirt. They are the ones who take down those big thick books

about the PLANTAGENETS and the Peerage that no-body else bothers with, and prop them up conspicuously around their work area in the hope that some newcomer will ask them why. One suspects that they may be the very ones who stand in clumps and wave little British flags when the Queen of England comes to visit in our country, because, they will say with their noses in the air, "One does what is expected of one in the presence of family!"

The "BEWILDERED BEGINNER". These pitiful cases can be any age, any sex. Those of us who are experi-enced in this highly complicated and intellectual hobby (and *never* in our lives acted like they do anyway) will just have to tolerate them, I guess. You can spot them right away. They park their cars in the spots reserved for staff, don't even know about signing the sign-up sheet, for heaven's sake, and bear the look about them that makes one wonder how they were ever able to find the library or archives in the first place without a personal guide. And their period of adjustment can run a long time. Some beginners stay that way forever. Why, I met one the other day who had been a beginner for 15 years! She didn't even know what a family chart was, if you can believe that, and just sat there with a completely blank look on her face when the library attendant asked her to produce hers. Since there aren't always paid staff members, or even will-ing unpaid volunteers, to assist these helpless neophytes, they can usually be guaranteed to latch onto a busy, knowledgeable veteran like yourself and expect help. Being greenhorns, they are always absolutely unprepared —no briefcases or nothing! They claim their grandfather's name was Smith (they don't even have enough sense to know that one always *capitalizes* surnames!), they think, and he came to the United States sometime between 1850 and 1930, but they don't know where he landed or where he settled and would you please find him preferably that morning because they have a baby-sitter waiting at home. You patiently ask for additional facts. They go into a deep study, ponder awhile, and finally offer the brilliant testimony that their grandfather, or was it their great-grandfather(?), they're not sure, was named either John, William or James and that his wife's name may have been Mary or Elizabeth. That's it! They wonder why everyone else is busy writing down things and why it all seems so difficult. Suddenly you are very thankful you brought along an extra supply of Anacin and, indeed, before this encounter is finally over with, you may be tempted to badger Mr. PEABODY (who is over in the corner in his customary alcoholic haze, trying to focus on the pamphlets) for a nip at his flask. You will need all the support you can come by in dealing with this dad-blamed nuisance (the beginner, not Mr. PEABODY).

The "OLD MASTER" or (if you will excuse the term) "OLD MISTRESS". You certainly ran into your share of this irritable breed when you were just starting the hobby. Most of them resemble sullen, retired school teachers. They are totally in control of their "own" tables and projectors and, since they consider themselves privileged individuals, they expect to be let in before opening time so that they can get to them. If you make the dastardly mistake of asking them a simple question, like, "Where can I find the 1890 census?", they look at you like you are not paddling with both oars. They cannot seem to understand or accept the fact that you want to start with your furthest-back ancestor, because you heard that your grandfather was just a farmer, or something equally as dull, and you would really be more interested in finding out if you are descended from King Henry VIII maybe, or someone a little more colorful. They treat that idea with a haughty sneer and huffily declare that if you don't do things their way, which is *The Right Way,* you haven't a tinker's chance of success. Additionally, some sure-fire ways to drive these old-timers into a raging fury is to not rewind your films, to turn on the lights in the projector room, or to have the unmitigated audacity to select a projector they think of as their own personal property. To further humiliate you, when whispering amongst themselves, they throw around a lot of meaningless initials, like IGI, GSU and LDS, and unintelligible terms, like "microfiche" and "lineage" to show their superiority and so you won't know what they are talking about. Well, in years to come you will certainly remember their degrading conduct, that's for sure, and when you finally join the upper echelons, known as "Experienced", you will *never* be observed behaving like those peevish, overbearing grouches.

The "UNCONSCIOUS MOTHER HEN". Actually this foggy specimen can also be a rooster, so to speak, but mothers generally predominate. Now your average well-balanced genealogical hobbyist, while fanatically, almost maniacally zeroed in on *family,* is very rarely ever caught red-handed with any live ones in a research center. Maybe that's because they tend to hit the age range between fifty and eighty, so have none left in the nest. But, unfortunately, there exists the occasional younger species, accompanied by a scruffy band of live progeny. Looking back, when you raised your own dear children, you were always, by golly, in complete command and the little darlings bloody-well behaved, or else! Not so with these modern breeders. They absent-mindedly sleepwalk through research facilities in the same befuddled fashion as they do every day in the supermarkets, other stores, buses, the movies, anywhere. The minute they come in the door they go unconscious, at least unconscious to the fact that they

brought in or are connected in any way to the band of little monsters tearing up the place. To alleviate this aggravating situation, each research center should install a sturdy receiving cage near the door and all humans under the age of 20 should be checked into it, the same as purses are checked into a locker. Otherwise we will all continue to have to endure small, uncontrollable offspring of this type whirling around in the aisles, whining in their shrieky little voices about offensive subjects like the availability of toilets and about everything else that happens to flit momentarily into their limited attention-spans, trying to look at the library books with their sticky, grubby hands, or committing the truly unforgiveable sin of actually taking over a chair and projector which, as everyone knows, should only be used by grownups. Libraries and archives will just have to set a rigid new rule: "Dead Relatives Only" or, at the very least, maybe a slightly less restricted one: "Adult Relatives Permitted", because, while prede-cessors are fine, little bitty descendants have no place in a family genealogical environment.

Now that you've been exposed to some of the draw-backs you will be associating with in your chosen hobby, we'd best get on to the next unpleasant topic about *Those Who Do It For Money,* and you can probably guess what *they* are called!

Mercenary
Researchers

Every genealogical researcher, at one time or another, will find himself or herself at the mercy of these hired hands. Unless you are very well-to-do, retired, and can drive to every county in the United States, or sail or fly to every foreign country where your family settled for a time, or may have settled but you aren't sure, you could be forced to take this sometimes unpleasant, costly route to obtain your family records. As one example, perhaps you have tried sending a simple request to a certain county courthouse, asking for a copy of a marriage certificate. That should be easy enough for even a county employee to find, you figure. You've told them it might have taken place between 1860 and 1880 (you're guessing, of course, because actually you haven't the foggiest notion of the date or even the state where said parties were married, or if they were married at all, quite frankly, but it's worth a try). You further caution the county clerk that the groom's surname can be found spelled 95 different ways, so you hope they won't overlook any possibilities. Well, wouldn't you know it would be just your luck that the county clerk in that particular location is extremely unco-operative, for some strange reason, and seems to want to do as little work as possible. You receive a curt answer suggesting you use a paid researcher (list enclosed). You have a strong suspicion that the "list enclosed" is made up of unemployed relatives of the reluctant county clerk, but the infernal place is 3000 miles away and your research will come to a screeching halt unless you can check the court documents in that secretive county seat. So you're stuck!

Another reason you might have to fork over some of your hard-earned money to a mercenary has to do with the simply maddening rules and regulations which certain fussy counties impose. In these high-handed jurisdictions, one or more power-happy elected officials has decided that what is best for the public is to keep the pesty souls as far away as possible from the public records. They believe that the best public record is one which is filed away in its proper niche, never to be seen again, or touched, or pulled out of place. As far as your impudent request that they actually *Xerox* a public record, well you'd as soon expect them to Xerox their private parts! After the proper interval of time, about two months or more, you will get a snippy little form-letter from this incensed county clerk, advising you that, if you persist in your demand to ferret out the contents of that specific document, you will have to resort to hiring the services of a paid typist (list enclosed).

The only other reason for hiring a paid researcher, that I can think of, is if you are really determined to do your family history but you can't sit still too long, and furthermore, you hate to spend too much time in stuffy, confined old places where official records are kept, then you may need to be serviced by a mercenary. These poor souls are surely the same kind of oafs who buy and eat already-prepared, frozen dinners and who own automobiles with automatic shift and cruise control. They are probably descended from the men who paid other poor devils to serve in their place in the army. For this irresponsible and somewhat peculiar "genealogist", there are plenty of folks ever so ready to take your money and send you most anything.

Having established possible reasons for resorting to such money-wasting activity, let us now examine the various classes into which your professional (and I use this term with a great deal of unbridled laughter) researcher might be placed. The following types are drawn from my own personal experiences (and after this book is out they will probably never answer my letters again):

The "RARE FIND". Sometimes I have the feeling that this exceptional couple never did exist at all, but were a figment of my imagination, a wild desire for the perfect paid researcher. They were an elderly couple (I deduced this fact because of the very feeble, though entirely readable handwriting and from their own admission that they performed this service to supplement their retirement income in a poor county where even the richest was judged to be not very affluent by national standards). They did a number of projects for me over a long period of time, were amongst the most prompt I had ever dealt with, and typed all information they gathered. Each packet of their work rarely cost over their $10 fee and occasionally they would return $5 of the payment with a claim that the results of an assignment were not worth the whole $10. A much later check of their record-gathering by another family researcher who visited that particular courthouse proved their top-notch accuracy. I know you are going to accuse me of nibbling on loco weed or being under the influence of some other substance and making up this couple in my delirium, but they really *did* exist. Also in this category, over the years, were others just as accurate, costing a bit more perhaps, but who provided prompt work worth what they earned. (I've put all this in here so that those who are still working for me, or who I hope to use in the future, will think I'm referring to them, or that they feel certain they will be placed in this classification—fat chance!) As far as the rest of them, it's all downhill.

The "DISCONNECTED". At the other extreme was the pathetic librarian who, I later figured out, must have been floundering around in the more advanced stages of mental impairment. Her work could very easily be divided into good and bad, with not much emphasis on the former.

In the "good" column was the fact that she typed whatever it was supposed to be and that it somehow got to my address. The "bad" classification covered just about everything else she did because it took her forever to complete what, for some unknown reason, she thought of as the assignment. Unfortunately, her completed work had no recognizable format or organization and was quite often not even about *my* family at all. She once sent a bunch of what appeared to be land records, as near as I could guess, for a name not in any way resembling the surname I had asked her to research (and I suspect, if she had actually found similar records for *my* ancestors, that she probably mailed them off to another equally puzzled and perturbed client). When I returned one whole packet to her, the contents of which I couldn't decode, and requested an explanation, she never referred to the matter again. Needless to say, I didn't authorize her to undertake any subsequent projects, but I did spend a very long and vexatious time urging her to complete my initial request or to refund a portion of my money, neither of which she ever did. Quite awhile after I had finally given up on her, that particular county office was still recommending her as a big help to researchers.

The "SCRIBBLER". You have all come across what you would readily identify as the very worst examples of atrocious handwriting (I'm married to one, but that's beside the point). Most of you have found these in census listings and county court records. But can you imagine a paid researcher who could easily duplicate their abominable style? To make matters worse, he's a dear sweet man (I met him once), a very thorough and knowledgeable professional genealogist who has access to a wealth of information in one of the nation's prime locations. But his handwriting is horrible! Certainly he is very prompt, does or tries diligently to do whatever he's asked, and sends huge packets full of well-organized papers, obviously full to the margins with Very Important Stuff, but it is in scribble that is easily inferior to my 4-year-old grandson's very best efforts. So you're forced to get out the old magnifying glass, ask everyone within hailing distance what some of the words look like to them, and gradually, word-by-word, decipher each of his papers into whatever it might possibly contain, maybe. Now and then I have tried diplomatically to suggest the use of a typewriter, even if I had to rent him one, but he can read his writing just fine, so doesn't see the need. Quite frankly, there should be a requirement nationwide that is strictly observed . . . if you don't have access to a typewriter, don't become a mercenary researcher!

The "BLAME-IT-ON-THE-WEATHER". Those of us who are blessed (some of you would say cursed) by being Californians have very little patience with the paid researcher in Minnesota, Indiana, Vermont, or other places where they have such peculiar weather and are always belly-aching about it. So you'd best be well prepared, anytime from September to June, to hear the tiresome old excuse for their slowness being that they can't get to the blooming courthouse because of the snow or ice or sleet or hurricane warnings (even though they always seem to be able to get to the bank to cash your check).

Out here in the "Golden State", we can drive two hours in the tule fog, through grid-locked traffic composed mostly of illegal aliens taking their first driving lessons, over-turned toxic chemical trucks, airplanes landing on the freeway, wrong-way drivers trying to commit suicide, daily protest marches, and Cal-Trans crews preparing to close down lanes for the construction of more lanes. Why is it then that, let a little snow fall back East and the whole place closes shop? I can understand how a paid researcher, or anyone else for that matter, might experi-ence some difficulty doing cemetery searching in a bliz-zard, or with the wind-chill factor down to 40 below and snow up to their clipboards, even if they have a sturdy shovel and a good sense of direction. But don't they heat those courthouses back there, or what? The best advice in dealing with that whole part of the country is to send your requests only in July and August, unless they are having a tornado.

The "PROCRASTINATOR". This person is relatively speedy in answering your initial inquiry asking about her fees, her current schedule, the procedure she proposes to follow, and her ability to tackle your job right away (which she insists she can do). But once you have sent her your request, accompanied by your check, she suddenly becomes totally bogged down. If it isn't July or August, she comes up with the "weather excuse" (see above). Other justifications given for her delay are: she's moving, she died, someone close to her died, she has made an immediate transformation from being an exceptionally healthy person to becoming hopelessly bedridden, her car has been stolen by a roving gang or is in the repair shop awaiting a rare part from overseas, she now has a backlog of 317 other requests ahead of yours, and on and on and on. . . . It was once my rotten luck in one county to discover three consecutive researchers all fitting perfectly into this designation until, when nearly at my wits' end, I was finally rewarded with one of the "RARE FINDs". I don't know what causes the "PROCRASTINATOR's" sudden lack of interest and initiative, usually occurring right after they have cashed your check. Perhaps they have better things to do with their time than to trudge off to the courthouse? Maybe they have gotten in a sudden feud with the County Clerk, or just simply lost interest in genealogy? Any of these reasons could account for their lethargy. If you find yourself dealing with many of this type, you will become proficient in composing pleading, coaxing and, finally, downright threatening letters in an attempt to goose them into the action that you have long since paid for. Good Luck!

So much for the irritating hangers-on you will be helping to support. For those beginners who haven't decided by now to switch to stamp-collecting, stealing hub-caps or some other hobby where you can see faster results, let us plod onward, from people to places.

To Get a
Whopping Headache —
Try the
National Archives

Are you ready to get initiated into the thrilling adventure awaiting you in the National Archives? I don't advise tackling the main one in Washington, D.C. if you are a timid beginner. In the first place, you might get trampled by the Old Guard when the officer-in-charge announces "opening time". But, if you're bound to ignore my warning and bent on conquering those hallowed halls, be prepared for what you will face!

If you make the trip to our nation's capital and want to stay in a hotel close to the Archives, you had better be in the same income tax backet as J. Paul GETTY, or plan to spend about three years' wages. Otherwise you would do well to locate in a slightly cheaper hostel in Virginia or some other convenient nearby state. Of course, then you will have to contend with the nightmare commute in rush-hour traffic, if you want to arrive when the Archives opens, from wherever you are to downtown Washington, D.C. on unfamiliar freeways. This harrowing experience might not faze you if you happen to be a Demolition

Derby driver, but any other occupation will not help you much. If you and your car are successful and eventually, after two hours or so in low gear or standing still, you get to the downtown area alive and are, hopefully, headed in the right direction on the one-way streets, your next task will be to figure out where to leave Old Betsy (your car, not your wife). Unless you want to run out and move it all day, you will have to settle for a parking garage. Bring plenty of cash in large denominations (which should make you popular with the resident muggers) so you can bail it out when you decide to leave, and jot down directions as to where you left it or you might never find the old crate again. If you are still in control and reasonably upright after you have left your car, you'll have a good, brisk, *long* walk across damp, muddy or snowy meadows and busy streets toward your goal. If you don't want to be mistaken for a tourist, don't look startled or pay even the slightest attention to any bodies you might encounter lying on the sidewalks. They are probably not dead anyhow, so just give them a wide berth, avert your eyes and keep going. I'm sure the ones who are still living do it on purpose, just to cause trouble. The authorities will eventually run them off, or have them carted away, before you come out again, so the sidewalks will be clear.

Once you are safely through the granite porticoes, you will find yourself in a kind of Official Interrogation Room where you must fill in a Government Form to prove that you are who you are and, if you pass this test, you will be issued a badge so that you can prove who you are all day. Security is very important there (especially if you are British with matches or a cigarette lighter, see later). They may even have started frisking people by now, especially the younger, prettier ones. Outside one room, when we were there, you were required to check the bulk of your clothing, all knapsacks, purses, briefcases, sack lunches, and any other portables excluding your own body, into a locker before they would allow you to go in the room. And a mean looking guard inspected everything you tried to take out of the room. So, if you plan to heist Grandfather's original Civil War file, the dusty old census books, or that quaint antique chair you've been sitting on, forget it!

Most visitors scamper directly upstairs to the projector room which, as I remember, was on about the fourth floor, a dark, semi-dark, or way-too-light world of constant spinning motion, strange clicking noises, flashing lights and very little assistance. Since your ancestors are in there someplace, you'll just have to adjust as best you can. The first annoyance you might encounter is the constant war which goes on between the lights-on faction and the lights-off gang. Now I don't mean to imply that the general public can expect to gain access to the master control for the light switches, the location of which is a closely guarded secret (except in the local Archives branch where I've discovered the controlling switch and flick it off as often as I dare), but they can sure create havoc with the curtain pull-cords. Suddenly everything becomes as bright as day and the faint, barely readable film you've been perusing goes completely invisible when these fiends fling the portieres wide open. Your best counter-attack in anticipation of this threat is to select a projector next to the curtain pull-cord and give menacing looks to anyone who approaches. Usually these curtain-openers are operating under the delusion that they can't see to walk around or read the indexes in a darkish room and that is what prompts their churlish behavior, but they should learn to see in the dark or bloody-well stay home! The aisles are always cluttered with them anyway, wandering around, half blind, or just standing in your way trying to get their bearings. The funny thing, though, is that they behave exactly the same way with all the curtains open. What we really need is a test administered at the entrance to the Archives to keep all confused people out.

Another needed regulation, which should be put into effect immediately, would save us all a lot of shoulder strain and subsequent cortisone shots. I propose that fingerprints be recorded, mug-shots be snapped and an oath be signed by each potential projector-user that he or she promises always to rewind their film. The penalty for breaking this pledge would be instant incarceration in a small, stuffy converted storage closet nearby, containing one projector and one chair, where the miscreant would be forced to wind the crank continuously for three hours or until he or she fainted, whichever came first. For who amongst us has not uttered colorful phrases when finding a roll of film (usually the fullest ones, at that) backwards, because some cretin has left it that way. Once I even came across a film that was inside out! Now *that* took some doing!

When we visited the National Archives there were, unbelievably, some raw beginners loose in the facility! They were looked upon by the rest of us with a great deal of pity because the poor misguided rookies were under the ridiculous impression that they would find help there. And, in fairness to the staff (because someday I may want to go back there and be let in), I did hear one or two employees telling the public where to go. But the vast majority of them were engaged in what they obviously considered much more important activities, like chatting with each other about the exciting aspects of their past and future social engagements. Anytime one of them sat down at a

desk, a line would immediately form of people with questions. But, if the line could be kept moving slowly enough or not at all, most of the questioners would eventually drop out due to leg-cramps, dizziness or compound discouragement. Another one of their obviously enjoyable duties, which they performed with great relish, was running folks off the projectors when the place got busy (citing as their reason a stupid two-hour usage rule thought up by some government sadist). For some of the employees, I suppose, it may have been the only taste they would ever have of unbridled power, and you could easily sense the satisfaction and wide grins when it came their turn to force a little old lady (me) to surrender her prized machine to an impertinent late-comer, a power-play they repeated as often as possible.

Since it may be a mystery to the non-genealogist (although whether anyone so labeled would have plodded this far into this book, or picked it up at all, is doubtful) about what could possibly be in the Archives in the first place to tempt so many folks there, like lawyers to a disaster scene, an explanation is necessary. For the dedicated genealogical researcher, the ultimate in excitement can be found there—census films, old military and pension files, and ship passenger lists. I discovered my maternal grandfather may have been a bigamist in that room! Well, now, I don't mean he actually accomplished the act within those four walls, because I think he did it in New York City, possibly in the back room of a saloon, but I learned the shocking news there! Other junk is stored in the building too, but it's mostly from and all about our Presidents, qualifying it in most folks' minds as too boring to waste time on.

Spending hours and days and years looking at census films can alter your personality forever and ruin your badly deteriorating eyesight in the bargain. Fortunately (as of this writing), any census listings more recent than 1910 are still kept secret and off-limits, and most states didn't commence their official snooping around much before 1800, if that early. They were too busy killing the people who lived here before them and anyone else who irritated them. States to the west, made up of folks who could no longer stomach the East, got an even later start because folks thought they could get out of paying state income tax by heading into the wilds and keeping it that way as long as possible. And, alas, thanks to that despicable band of early-day English terrorists, who were nothing but a bunch of unruly arsonists duded up in red blazers who got their kicks setting fire to our capitol buildings, some of those earliest census efforts and most of the Revolutionary War military and pension records went up in smoke. It was probably their way of getting back at us for winning the previous war. To this day, whenever I am in the vicinity of a British person, I get the strong urge to kick him in whatever protuberance is handy! Then, later, someone else, I think (or maybe it was a leftover Englishman?) set fire to the 1890 census, so that's another one we don't have to worry about.

I don't know if census takers ever had to take a handwriting test. Of course, in many counties in the early days, it may have been difficult enough even to find a man who could read at all, who possessed a reliable horse and the type of crops and wife he could leave unattended long enough to enable him to ride out and gather up the information. To be employed as one of the very earliest census enumerators was a snap: if the Indians didn't get you all you had to do was write one name at each log cabin. The rest was easy, just little x's or numbers or your own little inventive mark, reasonably near to, or in, the correct column for the few necessary questions. If you left out marks, or put them in the wrong place, so what! If you didn't ride out to some farms at all, because you had a feud going with the owners, who'd be the wiser? But by 1850, the Government meant business and it got pretty complicated and you couldn't bluff your way through the job so easily. Some census takers got stubborn or (more likely) couldn't figure out the fool government directives about how to be a census taker, so they took what is called the good old American initiative and did things their own way, with both positive and negative results. Some added the county name to the state name for each listee's birthplace, which is, for today's researcher, like finding an added, unexpected present under the Christmas tree. But the ones who really raise my hackles, my ire, and anything else that will go upright, are those imbeciles who decided to use only initials in place of the given names of the folks listed. The problems multiply in the instances where these lazy souls also neglected to fill in the sex of the initialee. I've found whole counties this way! Damn fools!

Bad spelling can be excused. After all, even our great Abraham LINCOLN's name was misspelled on the 1850 census. They spelled 'em how they heard 'em, and that was that! But what in the world did some of them use as writing instruments, anyhow? Either they were too timid to bear down hard enough to leave a lasting impression, or they distilled their own poor quality ink, which faded, or used some kind of homemade pencils. Many of the filmed records of their work are almost totally blank, or so faint and washed-out as to make the end result worthless. But, in fairness, I don't know enough about the process involved to be able to point the finger of blame for these disasters—was it the actual census employees or was it the later photographers who were careless with their focusing, who knows?

If you have never had the thrill of sending to the National Archives for copies of your ancestor's military and pension files, you should really give it a try. I could hardly contain my patience during the two months I waited for my first record of this sort. I just *knew* my relative, who had served in the Union Army in the Civil War and somehow managed not to get killed, must have performed countless valiant and dangerous deeds, while seriously wounded, at least, and probably received the highest medals and personal commendations from President LINCOLN himself in that bloody war. I could hardly wait to get the official confirmation of all this bravery and maybe frame it and hang it in a prominent place on the wall for all to see and envy. The day finally arrived when I pounced on the mailman who was waving a yellow packet in the air, full to bursting with our family heroics, I just knew. But now I'm not so sure. Should I frame and hang on the wall a communique bearing the impressive War Department seal that says our relative suffered from almost constant diarrhea, that his only wound happened when he hit himself in the leg with an ax when he was sent out on wood-chopping detail, and that he got measles while recovering from the self-inflicted ax-wound, which caused him to walk funny the rest of his life? But you've got to give the fellow credit, even with all the above hardships occurring in his first 3-year enlistment, he did his patriotic duty, hobbled up and re-enlisted in 1864 after completing all that near-heroism. I don't know, maybe his honors and decorations just got lost in transit.

This initial exploratory dip into the military records whetted my appetite to go full-speed ahead and send for copies of the Civil War and Revolutionary War files of every other relative on our family tree that I could connect to those national conflicts, desperately hoping to find a hero. While none of them proved to contain meritorious certificates from either Presidents WASHINGTON or LINCOLN, or anyone else very high in charge, they did divulge hitherto unknown and historically powerful information about my various family members dying of typhoid, lying about their age, losing their pension certificates, being taken prisoner, and not being very adept at ducking Minié balls. While we're on this subject, anyone dabbling in the pension files soon discovers that government red tape is not a modern invention but was fairly rampant as far back as shortly after we shook ourselves free of those infernal British (in fact, we probably learned it from them). One of the first matters of business, before the Revolutionary War muskets had hardly had a chance to cool down, was the originating of our very own Government Form, primitive ancestor to the vastly more complicated ones which drive us frantic in modern times. Reading through all those heart-breaking, begging appeals from shot-up veterans or their next-of-kin clearly shows that the Department of the Interior saved thousands of dollars on the pension funds it deliberately avoided paying because of its amazing ability to outlast potential applicants, their widows and offspring, and that same "Waiting-It-Out" mastery, as you well know, is still in practice down to the present day.

Before we leave the subject of the military and pension records, I have a word to say to all of you who are sitting out there with smug, know-it-all looks on your kissers, harboring the misguided notion that *you* wouldn't waste your time going in person to the National Archives for your family's military information because you have taken care of all that in a much more efficient manner, by sending for it through the mail. Well, I have the last laugh on you poor simpletons! What process of selection do you think those clowns back there employ to decide what papers out of your grandfather's file to send you? Eeney-meeney-miney-moe, that's how! Of course if you ask them, they will manage a serious proclamation, "We go through the file carefully and pick out all papers of a genealogical nature, copy and forward those." Balder-dash! In two separate, original files in Washington, D.C., for which we had previously requested copies and received by mail, we discovered what we considered to be items of a pretty significant tinge indeed, genealogically speaking, neither of which had been included in the assortment mailed to us. One was an original marriage certificate for a second marriage. The other was also a marriage record for a Civil War soldier who had been killed just months after his honeymoon and who none of our present family knew had ever been married at all. So now on those long winter nights, when you have plenty of time to ponder uneasily on the possibility, those of you who *think* you have all the information out of your family files back there can just wonder forevermore what family gems are still hidden away that you'll never find out about. Heh, heh, heh!

Whoops! Forgive me for becoming so emotional. Now that I've calmed down again, we'll get on with it. . . . Your ancestor may not have been lucky enough to have been blown away in our own Civil War, because he may have been doing his fighting amongst the peasants of Europe or elsewhere at the time. If he was and if you have any idea about what date he stopped playing soldier or digging potatoes or whatever he was doing in the Old Country and fell for some fast-talking promotional spiel, luring him over here to the Promised Land (or what date he got shang-haied, perhaps), you will want to ignore the census films in the projector area and head directly for the back room or wherever it is that they now stow the passenger-ship files. You will have to be almost fanatically determined in order to summon up the endurance necessary to wade through this type of search, especially if you are not too sure of the name your ancestor may have used when he arrived or the exact date he landed. Spending much time looking through passenger indexes and lists, I learned, is enough to send the average researcher racing full-blast to the nearest tavern. Those European ship captains and our domestic immigration authorities were not always too careful about what they did with the records they took or may have been given. Probably thought once they got the infernal foreigners over here, their job was ended, so they just turned the manifests over and used them to write down their grocery lists or to draw maps on for strangers or something, because not all the ship passenger lists wound up in the Archives. Maybe they still exist in the Big Warehouse of Lost Records somewhere in Washington, D.C., along with everything else they seem to lose back there, but they sure aren't all where you can get to them now. Some of the ones which are available appear to have been filmed by an inebriate on a 3-day binge. The pages are cockeyed, out-of-order and occasionally ripped or with huge chunks missing. But, notwithstanding, some of you lucky folks will actually find your ancestors, bigamous and otherwise, on these films, and finds of this nature can be pretty exciting!

The copy I have, listing my possible bigamist Magyar grandfather, also records every other passenger on the boat, except the cows. It has a whole long revealing line about each one, including if they were insane and how much money each brought to start a new life in America. Everyone on Grandfather's boat claimed to be rational but few had more than the equivalent of what it would cost nowadays to buy a loaf of bread and a six-pack of beer.

Since there was no such convenience as Welfare for them to go on immediately and stay on the rest of their lives, like there is now, they must have possessed more than the average share of gumption. Another find was that each passenger listed a person in this country (quite often a relative) who said they had agreed to go their bail as a sponsor. In my case, this added name allowed me to hang another relative on the family tree.

After you have recovered from your trip to the Archives, if you still have any steam left, you might want to learn about the myriad number of county courthouses just sitting out there waiting for you to violate their sacred contents. So we'll lurch on to the next chapter.

County Courthouses — Burned Down and Otherwise

There are two ways of assaulting county courthouses, indirectly by mail or with a frontal attack in person, either of which may give you plenty of reason for an outburst of temper. The primary irritation is that you may never find two courthouses in the United States of America, or even in any one state, that operate under the same set of rules. In fact, even in one specific courthouse I have found two separate offices using operating procedures completely foreign to each other.

One spot we visited, which shall remain nameless, is a good example. On a lovely autumn morning my husband and I strode, in a businesslike manner, yellow legal pads at the ready, through the massive antique door of the first office we encountered in the dilapidated old building. A woman was standing behind the huge old-fashioned desk, the only one in the room, pouring coffee in a cup, then straightening her desk, then rearranging things in her desk drawers. No one else was visible and, since the door had made considerable noise when we opened it and neither one of us was so slight as to pass for invisible, we felt she realized we were there, standing directly in front of her. We proceeded to clear our throats and fidget audibly. Finally, when she was at last good and ready, the old battle-axe condescended to notice the two alien beings who were polluting up *her* office and said, "What is it you WANT?" as if our very intrusion was an act of effrontery on her person. We said we were aware that that particular county had old death records limited to a few specific years but we would like to see them, please. Well, it was like asking this harridan for a peek at her underwear! She said they only had death records for a *very* few years (an echo of what we had just finished stating) and that she *knew* we wouldn't find any family records in them and we were not allowed back in the vault where they were kept anyway, harumph! With that curt little speech it was obvious she considered the matter closed, that we were, then and there, dismissed and banished from her sight. Now that kind of attitude, while it probably would have worked on my husband, always has quite the opposite effect on me. Drawing myself up into my full pouter-pigeon stance, I demanded in a louder than necessary squawk that, as a member of the public, I insisted on seeing those *PUBLIC* records, period! My husband, not wanting to referee a bout between two huffy old broads, started to bolt for the door, but the female Adolph HITLER (her, not me) capitulated and stalked off into the vault. When she emerged from the inner sanctum, she handed the dusty old volume to my husband and all further conversation by her, which was as little as she could help, was directed to him.

In order to deny satisfaction to the dictatorial old bat, I was absolutely determined to find a family death record in that ancient book, whether I found one or not (if that makes sense?). So, instead of just checking the ones I came to check, my main surnames who I knew had lived there in that time period, I looked up every single blasted surname I could vaguely remember as being on our family chart even if I could make no connection for them at all to this part of the country. Sure enough, I finally found two who at least bore the same surname as my great-great-grandmother's second husband. So, for the express benefit of guess-who, I shrieked, "OH LOOK! Here They Are! Just What We've Been Looking For!" Alan looked completely puzzled at the surname I was pointing out in the time-worn index, but wisely and from past experience decided he had better humor me and go along with whatever it was I was trying to prove. So he asked the indignant but somewhat surprised woman for Xeroxed copies of the two death certificates. "We can't do *that here!*" she countered. "You'll have to go down the hall!" The only recognized arrangement that Her Royal Highness would tolerate, it turned out, was that Alan would be allowed to go to another office in the building where they did that sort of menial thing. He would actually be permitted to take the sacred book with him, but I would have to remain as her hostage until he returned it. When I was finally released from her custody, I triumphantly marched out of there with the two death records of two people I'd never heard of in my hand and a smug smile on my face. I had won! At least I think I had. (A happy postscript concerning those two records came about a year later when it was discovered that both men turned out to be descendants of my great-great-grandmother and that they had previously been lost to family researchers because no one knew where they had moved. If the confrontation hadn't occurred, they would have remained undiscovered.)

The last sight we had of the Controlling Force in that

county office was seeing her seated on her throne, surrounded by two or three local judges, who had been sum-
moned to her office to discuss firing another employee.
"Discuss," I'm sure, was not the proper word because she
was, in reality, *telling* them she intended to fire the person
and they were nodding approval in unison, like those little
plastic birds with bobbing heads that some people used to
put in the back windows of their cars. So much for who
runs that county!

Next we went down the hall to the County Recorder's
office, where the offensive Xeroxing had been allowed to
take place, me with ruffled feathers, fully prepared for
another battle over their restrictive rules, only to be immediately calmed down and delighted at the entirely different
atmosphere. A smiling face greeted us (as my husband
assured me would be the case), belonging to one of the
nicest, most helpful and efficient county officials, as it
turned out, that we would ever meet. (I sincerely hope *she*

wasn't the one the other one wanted to fire!) She said of course we could go back into the room where the old record books were kept. She added that we could look through them alone or she would assist us if we preferred. She said to just come and ask her if we had a question. As a result of her kindly approach, we uncovered numerous family records, and that county probably took in more revenue off us than it did from traffic tickets the whole month after her stint at the copying machine. Toward the end of our stay in her office, she told us that she had phoned an elderly local gentleman who was considered sort of the unofficial county historian and asked him to come down and talk with us. She said he could answer any further questions we might have about early happenings and about the people in the area (which he did, even telling us where certain ancestors were buried). Every so often you will find a jewel amongst the brambles. If there are ever Genealogy Medals handed out. that rare lady in that second office deserves one.

There still exist in this country county offices which honor what you beginners expect to take for granted, the premise that public records ought to be allowed to be perused by members of the public. Others wouldn't hear of it! One example which comes to mind was in a location way out in the boondocks, where the county seat was composed of a silo, a service station that looked closed, one small grocery, what appeared to be a high school, a cafe, a church and the courthouse. It wasn't too difficult to determine which was the courthouse and to find parking right in front of it. The County Clerk's office was up a high flight of stairs, in a high-ceilinged room, with the highest counter I've ever seen blocking off the entire front of the room. That counter was so tall, almost shoulder-level, that at first we didn't even see the short, fluttery female it concealed. After we did, and gave her our reason for being there (a reason I don't doubt she immediately guessed, because, in a town of that size, she probably knew everyone in the whole area and their business as well), she informed us that they had one main rule in that office— *NO ONE WAS ALLOWED BEHIND THE COUNTER* (except for her, obviously). Freely translated, this meant that she would have to do all the research work herself. She was all alone back there, she kept telling us, and it was not supposed to be that way, she sighed, because she normally worked in the office down the hall, but Adelaide had to go to the doctor for a hernia (small wonder!) and Gladys' pickup truck had broke down (presumably leaving Gladys out there on the prairie somewhere, stranded), and she was doing the best she could, etc., etc. Seldom had we ever met such a highly nervous individual who was also infected by a good strong case of slowness, the two conditions usually being somewhat at odds with each other, but she suffered from both.

Her idea of efficient procedure was for us to write down each request separately, after which she would go back with it, one notation at a time, to where the books were kept and see if that particular item was in the index. Then she would putter around, trying to locate the matching master volume, bring it out and go through the agonizing efforts of hefting it up onto the high counter for us to double-check the names, after which she would wrastle the huge book under the copying machine and then stagger back to the shelves with it, repeating the grueling procedure for the next request. Watching her struggles was almost too painful to bear. The first time she went through this ritual, my husband, with good manners drilled into his head since childhood, tried to leap to her assistance when she attempted to lift the first heavy book nearly over her head onto the counter. But she warned him, between gasps, that he simply was *not* allowed back there. We guessed that the absent Adelaide was merely the latest in a long line of hernia patients out of that office.

As you can imagine, we soon realized we were in for a long day, either that or give up entirely, but we had spent five days and come nearly 2000 miles to get to that early family location, so we just prayed that the poor woman wouldn't be wheeled out of there to go join Adelaide before she could get finished with our business. But, if things weren't bad enough, soon the problems multiplied. Locals, mostly attired in overalls, kept coming into the room to interrupt her thinking and her toting. One wanted to pay a speeding ticket. One said he had just been let out of jail and asked to sign some release forms. One needed a kind of permit related to raising or selling pigs. One turned out to be a judge, informally dressed in jeans though he was, and hot on the trail of the fellow who claimed he'd been let out of jail. And so on. Almost three hours later we wearily departed with one will, two marriage certificates, one land transaction, and matching headaches. The little lady behind the counter vanished, lowering herself onto a chair or passing out entirely. I'm not sure which.

She was, by far, not the only official we ran across who insisted on doing all the work herself. Fast workers are rarely afflicted with this insane desire, only the slowest of the slow. One such person who plodded along, never out of slow gear, also insisted on stapling all copies for a single item together in one gigantic mess. Since she made three sections of copy for each page and never trimmed any of the copy papers, on a document running six or more original pages you wound up with a creation which would perform exactly like an oversized kite when you stepped out of the courthouse with it into a high wind. Needless to say, if you were ever able to get it under control, it was impossible to read and far too ungainly to jam into a briefcase. Alan and I made two different trips to that courthouse and spent a good deal of our time, on both occasions, untangling ourselves from our family records and getting the various paper monstrosities unstapled with a minimum number of finger punctures, all the while accompanied by a considerable amount of highly colorful language flowing freely from both of us.

One fact you must be prepared to accept is that the majority of staff members employed in County Clerks' or Recorders' offices hate the very innards of all genealogists and, therefore, do not carry on too ecstatically when one of us approaches them in their territory. This goes triple for anyone from California, because folks elsewhere, for some reason, seem to be under the peculiar impression that our lovely state is populated by nothing but flakes.

While we're on that subject, I spent two research vacations trying to explain our then-Governor BROWN's behavior *re* fruit flies, etc. to various county employees in other states (even though I could never figure it out myself), because they always asked, as if we were personally responsible for the fellow, and we hadn't even voted for him. So Californians would do better to park their cars down the street, or somehow cover their offending license plates, and pretend they are from Nebraska. If you are a genealogical researcher, though, no matter where you hail from, you had best come to grips with the realization that, as often as not, you will be glared upon as if you had just slithered out from under a rock. If the clerks are the female variety (and most of them you'll deal with seem to be loosely classed as such), it won't hurt to have your husband prostitute himself a little bit toward them. I'm not exactly certain that's the proper word (?), but he could at least try to leer at them like Clark GABLE in *Gone With The Wind*, pat them in an appropriate spot when they bend over the copying machine or otherwise give them the impression that he's nearly bowled over with lust at the sight of them. You *might* get better service as a result, if he'll agree to perform this service for you, especially with the older, uglier ones. But I'm not guaranteeing anything, you realize, because in these modern days with all sorts of radical new liberation notions floating around, they could take umbrage at him real quick. If that becomes the case, it's best for you to immediately act as if he is a total stranger, one who just happened to follow you in off the street. Now if you don't have a husband to pacify the cranky old gals in the courthouse, or you can't proposition a passing male to accompany you there for a few hours for that purpose, you will simply have to employ some other tack. You can always tell them, being careful to maintain a straight face if you can, that their office and the fine officials in it are just the most efficient, helpful and best organized in the whole United States of America. That will sometimes do it, if you can keep from erupting into laughter.

If you persist in this genealogy madness over a number of years or your husband, for some unknown reason, lays down the law about never going on another research trip with you, you may be forced to resort to writing to county courthouses instead of paying them personal visits. Or, if you are on your long-awaited and only research vacation and manage to arrive at a certain county seat at 5:05 P.M. on a Friday afternoon and can't stand the thought of wasting a whole weekend in that miserable, dull location, the mail may become your only source of communication if you decide to depart immediately for another county which might offer more action.

When you write to a county office with a specific request, don't ever trust them. The answer you receive could *possibly* be the truth, but it is more likely instead that the person receiving your request hates looking up things, has had a past grudge with someone bearing the same surname as yours, can think of more interesting ways to spend his or her worktime than messing around with the cumbersome old record books, or has very poor eyesight, so it becomes far easier to just write back that they can't find it (especially in those loathsome counties operating under the rule that they get to keep your check just for looking). Some clerks, I strongly suspect, are just plain sadists who get their jollies disappointing genealogical researchers. I make these accusations with a great deal of authority because two separate times in two separate states, I have caught them at it, so that should certainly prove it! Once they swore my grandmother couldn't possibly have up and died in the place I claimed she had, and after I'd sent the request to them three different times. I got so riled up, I drove down there in a huff and, minutes after entering said government facility, pointed an accusing finger at my grandmother's clearly spelled name right there where it was supposed to be in the proper record book, establishing beyond a doubt that she had breathed her last in their fair jurisdiction. Another time in another state, a lazy clerk sneeringly suggested that my great-grandfather's brother may have been too destitute to have left any kind of estate settlement in their specific locality. When I later visited the same courthouse in person and found a lengthy probate file for the gentleman, with no difficulty at all, you can bet they heard about it! So, my advice to you is never take "There is no such record here" as an answer.

Before we leave the subject of county courthouses, we should discuss their physical characteristics in order to get you further prepared. The first rule is "Never Laugh Uproariously At What You Find In Them!" This goes for people, things and the architectural layout, itself.

In the smaller burgs, the courthouse is easily recognized, usually, unless it has burned down. Then it could be most anything, even that crummy-looking quonset-hut with the flagpole out in front. A flagpole is often, but not necessarily, a dead giveaway in the more patriotic, conservative sections of the country where a fervid Republican tavern owner might even mark his business establishment in this manner (and when I finally found my husband inside, he tried to use the feeble excuse that he thought it *was* the courthouse). Anything that looks like it has been there a long time and is surrounded on four sides by the only commercial buildings for fifty miles, is probably the edifice you want. Most courthouses give the reassuring appearance of being there to stay, with a lot of granite or marble or concrete stairs going up and down, and ponderous old solid doors which undoubtedly caused many previous county officials terminal bursitis. Many of them have a peculiar musty smell to them (the buildings, not the officials, necessarily), but most of them are not too dirty. One county in Missouri must be blessed with towns-people who have just one recognizable and uncontrollable pastime, because every few feet in their courthouse the visitor is greeted with printed signs, all with the same admonition: "Don't Spit On The Floor!" This particular building was a fanatically spotless place, reeking of industrial-strength sheep-dip, and being kept that way constantly by a cleanup person on each floor toiling away with a mop and scrub brush and an ever watchful eye out for expectorators.

It is hard to know ahead of time what whims of fancy will dictate when the individual courthouses will be open each day for business and when they might abruptly close. To further complicate matters, renegade jurisdictions like Indiana make up their own rules about keeping time (I understand they stubbornly ignore the daylight-saving time the rest of the country knuckles under to), and it is not unusual for their outside clocks to be broken too (probably by an enraged out-of-state visitor on a rampage). Furthermore, don't be surprised to see unexpected or unusual items inside some courthouses. We could barely squeeze in the front door of one of them (again in Indiana—that state is a real puzzle sometimes!) because of some kind of tractor someone had parked just inside. I think it may have had something to do with snow and the lack of any place else to put it, or else the County Clerk was the local distributor for them, or there was a tractor crime-wave presently going on there, I don't know. By the way, when we came out of that courthouse, easing past the tractor, around noontime, the locals were running some kind of fire-drill around the square (at least we hoped it was a drill and not a real conflagration, or the stricken structure would have been a goner for sure). A group of men were trying to get the bright red firetruck, circa 1928, to go more than a few feet. The siren worked fine, to which everyone for miles around could heartily attest, I'm sure, but the truck itself wasn't doing too well. It would lurch forward a bit, accompanied by loud, exploding noises and then wheeze into silence once more. We watched the production while we ate our lunch on the courthouse lawn. Since they had gotten their monstrous charge crosswise in the middle of the main street, their futile activities were beginning to cause a traffic jam for the two or three pickup trucks trying to get to town. The last sight we had of the stalwart crew, they were attempting to relieve the gridlock by pushing the reluctant behemoth out of the way partly onto the sidewalk. I wouldn't want to sell fire insurance in that town!

Unless you are in good shape and can climb like a mountain goat, you may have to make some important decisions in the average courthouse regarding stairs. The ones you must use to get up to the front door in the first place, I can't help you with—you'll just have to negotiate them any way you can. But once inside, you can usually choose between an elevator and the grueling stairways. Many of the elevators look as old as the buildings housing them and don't exactly inspire much confidence. Once I saw a figure outside one of them I took to be a statue, but it turned out to be the elevator operator. He was, without a doubt, the oldest human being I'd ever seen. He made the Dalai Lama in the Ronald COLMAN version of *Lost Horizon* look like a teenager. Not wanting to find out, first hand, if he and the elevator would make it to the third floor, where the Clerk's and Recorder's offices were

located, we took the stairs. Coming down again later in the day, we probably should have hazarded a wild chance with the elevator because the interior of that building, unfortunately, was pretty much all the same color of white, and the previous week I had been newly intro-duced to bifocals. After hours spent reading old books and papers full of tiny, cramped writing, I couldn't differentiate between the stair-risers and  open space, with the result that I took a header into the rotunda, right on my clipboard. My husband, who embar-rasses far too easily, tried to act like he wasn't with me, which didn't set too well. The ancient elevator operator, probably determined to prove he was more agile than I was and perhaps deeply imbued with an old-fashioned sense of chivalry, proceeded to hobble over to come to my aid but, by the time he got there, I had hauled myself out the door, injured dignity, bent clipboard, black-and-blue marks and all. As for Alan, who by then looked suspiciously like he was about to break into a fit of hilarity, I took care of him by "tactfully" reminding him of his own clumsy fall right in front of the National Archives building in Washington, D.C., the nation's capital, for heaven's sake, and a far more shameful spot to pick for acrobatics. His fall there didn't differ from mine all that much except everything at that location was the same shade of grey, rather than white and, like me, he was becoming used to his own pair of bifocals at the time, so you would think I would get a little sympathy. The lesson here is, especially if you are older with brittle bones and don't bounce too well, watch where you step, and do it through the top half of your spectacles.

One thing you can't assume is that all courthouses routinely remain open from 8:00 to 5:00 every weekday except national or state holidays. They lock those doors every chance they get! Remember, no matter how small the county seat, those people in there are not regular workers, in the true sense of the word. You are dealing with honest-to-goodness, certifiable government employees! They learn fast! Working for any government entity equates to doing as little of it as you can get away with for as few hours or days as you can figure out. Why, they even expect duty-free lunch hours! Some counties go so far as to herd everyone outside, close down the entire courthouse and lock the front door when noontime rolls around so that most of the folks who punch the clock can amble over to the cafe and get them their victuals. It doesn't matter a bit if you are on a roll at the time, digging up family court records galore—out you go! You can either go to the cafe too, which can be quite an experience, or sit and stew. In other places the clerks cease talking to you at 12:00, right in mid-sentence if need be, pull out the plug on the copying machine, whip out a sack lunch and go sit down in the back room. All work, or whatever they call what they've been doing, comes to a grinding halt. You're so revved up and have driven so far to get there, you really don't see why they should indulge in such rude behavior as to take time out for food. It's downright inconsiderate when what you're doing is so highly important!

And it might be your luck to be confronted with even stranger scheduling scenarios before you are finished. We arrived in breathless anticipation, as one always does, in a Kentucky courthouse at 11:55 one morning and started to explain why we were there and ask about their procedure. The lady behind the counter said they were getting ready to close. Being an old hand who was used to lunch-time excuses at that point, I grinned knowingly and assured her that I understood and that we'd see her at one o'clock. She said something that sounded like, "Aowh no! We kuhwit fur the diay ayut tuhwelv. Doan nun uv us cum bayuck a'tawl ayftur thayut!" No wonder my family, who used to live in that county, took to using their guns to get anything done!

In the last few years some courthouse staffs have in-vented yet another sneaky trick to thwart you in your chosen hobby. They have *Sent the Records Someplace Else!* To justify their perfidious behavior, they will, of course, quote the tired old canard, "We did it to preserve them." Literally translated, this means they got rid of the pesky old records so that they could get rid of the pesky old record seekers. When you stop to think of it, that is a fool-proof way to keep what they consider despicable nuisances from loitering around underfoot in their court-houses, interrupting their leisure time with a lot of silly questions about people who died a long time ago. You can hardly blame them. But, somehow, having the ancient books transferred away from where they belong to imper-sonal, sterile films or microfiche and neatly stored some-place in the state capital just doesn't create the same feel-ing as walking into a courthouse where your predecessors actually may have walked, pulling down the dusty old volumes from where they've been stashed, getting you and your garments filthy in the process and nearly putting your back out from all the hefting, but emerging with an au-thentic handwrit record, by golly, and a well-deserved smile on your face. When you find something under those conditions, it's really worth it! But I'm afraid other coun-ties will soon adopt this sure-fire genealogist repellant and future researchers, denied the challenge of using them, will one day not even know what a courthouse is. But enough of nostalgia.

Because at the present time you are still allowed the use of them, after you have exhausted your patience and your pocketbook at the courthouse and gotten your eager hands on Xeroxed copies (readable and unreadable) of every act your ancestors committed which caught the fancy of the authorities of their time, you are next ready to beat a path to a place that shouldn't cost you so much, the nearest library. All you hope is that it has a genealogy section and that it's open.

The Hottest Hangout
in Town —
Your Library

I'm not about to poke fun at the LDS Genealogical Library in Salt Lake City, because they might strike my newly acquired family history from the shelves or send a hit squad, or not let me back in next time, so I'd better treat that place with the reverence it deserves! Besides, I've never quite gotten over the heady feeling most researchers experience when they go through those portals for the first time. It's like dying and being accepted straight into heaven! Even a whole week spent in an unyoked orgy amidst the stacks in Salt Lake City will not satiate one's thirst for digging up the dead-and-gone. For those of you lucky enough not to suffer car failure on the abominations Utah jokingly refers to as its highways and who actually reach 35 North West Temple Street, you will know what He meant when He said, "THIS IS THE PLACE!" You can wallow in books, films and microfiche about everybody's dead relatives up to your armpits and never exhaust it all.

So much for ecstasy. Now for those of you who break down in Evanston or Elko, or who are on a limited retirement income which doesn't permit trips much beyond where you can hoof it, you will have to make do with the libraries closer to home, and let's hope you know how to act in them! Missouri probably wouldn't hesitate to post signs enforcing library deportment (in light of their known spitters). California, at the other extreme, of course, is the recognized mecca for outlandish behavior, so don't expect any restrictions out here in Cuckoo Land. We rarely raise an eyebrow at anything weird at this point in time. Why, just the other day in a library in Monterey my daughter and I found ourselves sharing a table with a young man in jeans, tee-shirt and a long black cape. To complete his outfit, he had a sword strapped around his mid-section. My daughter, annoyed at me for glancing in his direction, whispered, "For heaven's sake, Mother, that's just a Renaissance Man," and we went on (me a bit nervously) with our research. But institutions in responsible states are not guaranteed to be so anarchic and may actually have regulations, even for eccentric Californians to observe.

Perhaps it is because librarians lack a certain sense of everyday excitement in their lives that gives them such a strong desire to cause some in yours if you flaunt their rules, and they have no shortage of those. Sometimes all it boils down to is the general admonition: "If you act up, you get tossed out!" Other places have a whole list of specific orders concerning library etiquette. Like "DO NOT RESHELVE THE BOOKS!" Librarians have been inoculated since their schooldays with the one-track notion that each book must be put in a certain pre-destined spot and that he or she is the only human being capable of performing this complicated feat. If you happen to wear thick glasses, act more than a mite confused, and attempt to do your own re-shelving, rest assured they will get especially testy and may even burst forth with a spontaneous lecture about the Dewey Decimal System and law-and-order.

If you notice a big sign conspicuously posted, "DO NOT TAKE GENEALOGY BOOKS OUT OF THIS ROOM!" and you forgetfully wander out with one to show Aunt Gertrude who is sitting in the Romance Section getting her jollies from the gothics, you might find yourself in manacles and headed for the station. If the copying machine is located in another part of that particular library, that becomes another cause for concern and it may be wise to obtain a written pass or risk sending the genealogy room attendant into a frenzy.

Libraries aren't intended as places for chatting with your friend Sandra about who you've found, who she's found, who each of you hopes to find, and what you are planning to cook for dinner that evening. Libraries are supposed to be synonymous with QUIET! For those of us who have reached a more responsible age (over 50) and have had drilled into us as children the iron-clad manifesto forbidding noise in such places, it isn't difficult to bend to the will of various persnickety librarians. But for the younger individuals, many of whom are nearly deaf anyway from constantly listening to that eardrum-shattering racket they have the impudence to refer to as music but which sounds more like someone killing cats, the adjustment may be impossible. Such little heathen lack the faintest idea that it isn't perfectly acceptable to carry on in a loud manner in libraries just the same as they do at the movies or anywhere else cursed with their presence. But, I will have to admit, some older folks don't behave much better. Maybe the solution to the problem would be a strict Library Gag Rule, printed on a card and quietly issued to each incoming patron, forbidding any talking at all. Breaking the rule would automatically unleash two monstrous men, perhaps ex-football players from the Los Angeles Raiders, who would then tackle the offender to the floor and place a real gag on the lower portions of his or her face. I'll bet it wouldn't take too many of such little disciplinary actions for patrons to seriously consider re-structuring their lifestyles, and blessed quiet would be restored to our libraries.

But what does one do for entertainment when one has just successfully piloted the family jalopy through 2315 miles of construction zones, cops hiding behind bridge abutments, lumpy-bed motels and ptomaine-dispensing eateries, only to arrive at that very special pioneer family location early on a Friday evening and then make the dis-covery that there is not even a library in the whole blame county. That being the case, how do you kill time the entire weekend until the infernal courthouse opens its doors on Monday morning? It is useless to try to find the family homestead spot, without a recorded land record, the likes of which are now concealed within that same tightly locked courthouse. What do you suppose, then, is tops on our list of suggestions for filling the intervening hours with excitement of the wildest kind? That's right! A fun-filled jaunt through the local cemeteries!

Browsing in Cemeteries

W hile perhaps not at the height of current fashion, the most practical ensemble for both male and female cemetery aficionados is the rain-slicker and wading boots, even on hot summer days, in fact, in any season but winter. For cemetery strolling in the dead of winter you might need to have your head examined so you can be fitted with goggles and a knit cap to complement your choice of snowsuit. A shovel is a must in winter, depending on the snow depth, and also, at times, for getting your car unstuck from wherever you frivolously parked it. However, I must urge extreme caution trying to take a shovel into a cemetery, as some nervous folks in the vicinity might misunderstand, and there is no sense spending your valuable time in the slammer.

Now I know heated arguments are bound to arise disputing my recommendation to wear rain-gear, mainly from those of you whose only contact with cemeteries has been to be forced to go to one for some less important occasion like a funeral. That is simply not the same as wandering around in one all day long. Fiendish cemetery employees turn the sprinklers on when you least expect it (I suspect they lie in wait to do it), but if you are costumed properly, you won't lose your composure and you will be able to slosh along undaunted. The illustrator of this book, not having made a habit of regularly doing his sketching in a cemetery, didn't heed my warning, thinking it just the ravings of an hysterical woman. Well, they saw him coming, and his sketch book is still in the process of drying out. Even if the sprinklers are not deliberately aimed to coincide with your planned arrival, they were probably turned on previous to it, because the grass is always sopping wet in cemeteries—you can count on it. If you try to take in a cemetery in the early morning on your way to a courthouse, as I frequently do, and you are not wearing waterproof kneeboots, you are going to look like you had a very peculiar accident by the time you arrive at the courthouse.

A procedural question confronts those engaged in this stimulating type of undertaking, one that is fraught with controversy. How does one properly walk in a graveyard? Oh, vertically, of course, but in between or over the top of? If it's someone else's family plot you're ambling through and you are in a hurry to find yours, perhaps it would be all right to cut across all those resting in peace, now and then, if other upright, live ones are not in the vicinity. But otherwise, and especially where it concerns your own dear ancestors, please show some respect and watch your step! Besides, with some of the older graves, quite often there is sinkage into which you could take a nasty nosedive, or you might find, on occasion, downright and unexpected cave-ins, so it's safer to avoid those spots. After all, there's no need getting there any faster than your appointed time.

In small country burial locations in conservative states you may encounter another problem, and that is contending with the neighbors who live next-door to the sacred old grounds. They always give the impression that they think you are up to something fishy (especially if you happen to be sporting what they consider proof of derangement in the form of California license plates on your car). They cannot seem to get it through their thick bumpkin craniums that there are lots of perfectly sane folks who just love to browse through cemeteries. Sometimes they'd as soon sic their dogs on you as to talk about it and, since most farm dogs tend to be big scary ferocious ones equipped with excellent sets of fangs, you had better be alert and swift of foot. It wouldn't hurt to do a spot check on the distance to the nearest handy tree designed with climbing possibilities. Or, if you consider yourself too dignified for, or inept at, tree climbing, you could always estimate the exact time it would take you to sprint from the graveyard back to your car by trying a few practice runs (drawing further knowing nods from onlookers).

If you are lucky enough to confine your escapades to city memorial parks with no threatening canines nearby or farmers on the prod, it may still be wise to observe certain civilized customs. Cutting up in a cemetery is usually frowned upon by most people of good breeding, and even Democrats too. My husband, about as staid, no-nonsense kind of guy as you can find, learned this little lesson the hard way. Right in the middle of one of our newly discovered family plots, doggoned if we didn't find ourselves staring at a gravestone with *his* name on it! Now such a discovery can calm a person down rather hurriedly, even if he isn't particularly riled up in the first place, and Alan was no exception, that is, for awhile. Then some irreverent person amongst us (my daughter claims it was me, but I don't believe that) suggested it would be funny to have Alan pose with the tombstone so we could snap a picture. While he outright balked at a prone position, he did consent to sitting alongside the tombstone with one arm around it, pointing to it with the other hand, all the while with a slightly giddy look on his face. That did it for my daughter and me! We broke up into a fit of laughter which encouraged Alan to pursue the rare (for him) spectacle of performing as a comedian by attempting to act like he was crying while embracing the grave marker, which activity only escalated our hysterics. Unfortunately, at this very pinnacle of our high-jinks, wouldn't you know,

there suddenly appeared on the scene a half-dozen somber looking folks carrying flowers and looking absolutely aghast (as well they should) at having witnessed such shocking shenanigans in a cemetery! So, if any of you has a warped sense of humor, it's best not to exercise it over someone's final resting place.

Other tacky cemetery behavior includes, in the rare instance when the grass is dry, spreading out a blanket and having a picnic lunch over the departed, or sunbathing on the blanket (or anything else you might think of doing on it), stealing flowers from someone else's grave to decorate your family plot because you forgot to bring your own, and any type of peculiar or noisy activities if a funeral is being celebrated nearby. Heaven knows, we will all be there ourselves someday and we would resent, just as much as the next fellow, someone's scatterbrained descendants frolicking and cavorting about out of control overhead.

If you ever have occasion to visit a national cemetery to try to find a Civil War soldier's grave (or any other military grave), please permit me a word of caution. It might be best to time your arrival to occur on a day and at an hour when the office on the premises is open so you can obtain a map. Because, unless you know *exactly* where the specific grave is located, you could easily become nauseated or delirious from wandering around hour after hour trying to read names from all those rows and rows of identical tombstones. Believe me, it is almost as dizzying as six straight hours of projector operating.

Now, a final bit of advice on this subject. . . . As you know, we genealogists, once set loose, closely emulate pack rats. Everything we find is carted home, if possible, including copies of anything we can jam under a copying machine, rocks from the family homestead property, pieces of wood from old houses, and anything else we can filch. In the course of our most frantic activity, we accumulate briefcases, cardboard boxes, filing cabinets, sometimes whole rooms full of all kinds of memorabilia, proof that our ancestors really did live, marry or carry on, die, and do other stuff. Most of this souvenir gathering, it is hoped, is fairly innocent and only causes minor damage. But please, *contain yourself in a cemetery!* What is in those places was meant to stay there! You can't take your newly discovered great-grandfather or his tombstone home for share-and-tell at your local historical society's next meeting. You can't even dig him up to make sure he's still there. Just be content to do a rubbing (of his stone, that is), or else copy the engraved information on your clipboard. And if the name is spelled funny, as ours usually is, for goodness sake, don't try to chisel a correction. It is probably considered sacrilegious at the very least to chip away, carve your initials, or otherwise mess around defacing the grave markers. Too many earlier scavengers have done their share of desecrating already, as you will notice. As a deplorable example, we learned that one of our ancestors tried to sell the family tombstones for a little extra spending money a long time ago. Nobody knows what happened to the stones in question when his contemptible scheme fell through, but that is a good illustration of misdirected pioneer ingenuity which causes present-day genealogists massive headaches. So, you had best treat the objects laying around in graveyards strictly off-limits as souvenirs.

Once you get the hang of this fascinating hobby and start pestering your friends with endless, spellbinding details of your daily progress, don't be surprised if they have to hang up for continual pressing emergencies when you phone them, or if they are always just leaving for an important engagement when you drop in to visit. Old buddies, who are not into genealogy themselves, seem to disappear like an endangered species when you no longer care to spend time gossiping about anyone but your long-dead relatives. So, unless you are a confirmed hermit, you will seek new pals, and there is a treasure-trove awaiting you, all of whom are hopelessly addicted genealogico-holics just like you. Go ahead, join the herd!

Enough Genealogical Societies to Choke You

I'm much too overweight to get into my old formal, haven't backcombed my hair in 20 years, and wearing sashes across my chest restricts my breathing, so I don't think I'll try to join the D.A.R. Besides, if that august body ever got wind of the "Criminal Records" section in my family history, they would never extend a membership invitation anyway. Our family stories claim our ancestor was a Frenchman who fought with LAFAYETTE in the American Revolution. But at this point in my research, I don't know if he just argued with LAFAYETTE, actually fought on the same side as that famous French hero, was in the army or navy, or what he was up to? I think he left France in a big hurry, for whatever reason, changed his name a lot after that, and had an aversion to courthouses or any other place where the authorities hung out and where he would be likely to get recorded as doing whatever it was he did, and I'm sure the D.A.R. would not be too receptive to that explanation. Of my UNDERWOOD ancestor, on the other hand, one story said that he fought at the Battle of Guilford Courthouse, which should qualify me right there for the D.A.R., except that, unfortunately, another version said that a tree fell on him. In view of certain later known activities within that branch of my family, I certainly hope he was not, at the time, attached to the tree by a rope. So, unless my research turns up something more enlightening (and acceptable), I guess the D.A.R. will just have to struggle along without me.

As I've heard tell, it used to be that the D.A.R. was a pretty loose organization. Don't get me wrong, I don't mean to imply by this statement that the ladies in it were loose (or at least I'm not aware that they were), but the regulations for joining that noble band were far too lenient for anyone's good. Why, certain cagey inveiglers padded their membership forms with absolute falsehoods and, as a result, you can't imagine what perfect scalawags sneaked into the royal circle!!! One cannot even begin to envision the horrendous punishment which must have been dealt out to descendants of these rascals once their true character became known. I'm sure their sashes were stripped right off them! But then, as time came to pass, those who had slipped in easily at the beginning (under those same slack, free-wheeling early membership standards) decided they were going to make their little club Ultra Exclusive and stop letting in the dregs. They tightened ranks like you wouldn't believe, so are no longer considered easy. At the present time, unless you are a direct descendant of George WASHINGTON (which any fool knows you couldn't possibly be), or have lots of time and moola to devote to proving a definite connection between yourself and one of those other troublesome fellows the British called traitors, you had better not try to infiltrate the D.A.R.

Luckily, for those of us who are unacceptable, there are loads of other genealogical societies who are not particular who they take, so long as you can come up with the yearly membership fee. It's OK by them if your ancestors were traitors (to *our* side) in the Revolution, peasants from Poland, horse thieves, or even illegal aliens. And, if that isn't enough to tantalize your appetite, some of these organizations offer further little rewards in the form of specially honored upward designations within the membership structure. Let's see if I can explain this rather complicated maneuvering. To be allowed into these favored positions, you must prove your ancestor, traitorous or otherwise, bought land in that specific political jurisdiction, or perpetrated some other little stunt by which he manipulated himself into the official record books (say, I wonder if they would count criminal records?) by a certain date, for which you are obligated to secure a Xeroxed, certified, stamped copy. After you are done copying it, notarizing it, and swearing to it, what you wind up with as a final result must be forwarded to the Official Decision-Making Board of Judges in Charge. Now this is serious business and said illustrious panel diligently studies every last morsel of your miserable offering, looking for cheating. They then ceremoniously pass judgment on whether you really did have an ancestor and whether he truly did live in, or do something that caught other people's attention in, that particular place before the Official Cut-Off Date for that sort of thing, or whether you are just trying to get away with something. If the Board, in its great wisdom, stamps you with its approval and blessing, then you get to pay more than other people to be a member of that society. Don't ask me why, but that's how it works. I'm not sure exactly what happens if they catch you red-handed in the act of submitting a forgery, or an improperly notarized piece of paper or some other type of heinous falsehood. If something blasphemous like that occurs, you are probably sent a very curt notice on official society stationery notifying you that you will only be permitted to pay the lower fee from that day forward, no matter how much you beg, and also spelling out a dire warning should you try anything else funny in the future. As a final act of humiliation, all society quarterlies subsequently coming your way will undoubtedly be stamped with a big red "A".

In case you haven't the foggiest notion what they actually do in these mysterious genealogical fraternities, most of them, in return for the yearly fee, send out some kind of mimeographed quarterly (with a cute name that somebody went to a lot of trouble to think up), unless the

editor is too busy, or dies, or has some other more important business to take care of that month. It is very exciting
to receive these quarterlies in the mail because someday
one of them might even contain your surname or something that will be of use to you in your research. Mostly,
though, they seem to be all about other people's ancestors,
but you never give up hope. One way to see your name in
the quarterly for sure is to send in a Query. If you're a
member, it only costs you a postage stamp and, who
knows, you might even get an answer to your Query,
although usually anyone who answers has more questions
than you have, sends information you've had for years, or
asks for your records for a book they are writing. The
classic example of tackiness we've all experienced in Query
response is the twit who writes, sends absolutely no family
information at all, asks for *all* your records, and has the
audacity to not even enclose a stamped, self-addressed
envelope (or SASE, as we genealogical experts call it).
Something like that will keep you steamed up for a week!

Another way you can insure that your name and that of
your ancestor get in the blooming quarterly is to submit
a fascinating story, written by you, of course, all about
your family. Just think how lucky they would be to latch
onto something like that! But, sad to say, this can be a
disappointing experience because, while you have every
reason to assume that your literary effort should have its
proper place as the lead article, or that they might even
devote the whole issue to it, seeing as how it turned out to
be 29 full pages of single-spaced, highly descriptive narrative about how your great-grandfather joined the army in
the Civil War and stayed in for 15 days until he decided
he'd had enough and it was time to go home and harvest
his crops. Pretty exciting stuff! But the editorial staff back
there, undoubtedly jealous of your superior writing abil-

ity, cuts and slashes your masterpiece unmercifully until it is just a tiny paragraph on page 35 and, to further insult you and your family, they even manage to spell your great-grandfather's name wrong! As a matter of conjecture, I don't think *I* would ever be faced with this kind of abysmal treatment, if I ever decided to send in a story, since I come from a long line of folks who didn't hesitate to pull a gun to right situations that didn't go exactly their way, but you more docile would-be authors might do well to heed the warning.

Even with a few annoying problems now and then with the quarterlies, most of them at least give you *something* for your money. On the other hand, there is an absolutely disgraceful squandering of membership fees that goes on constantly in the average genealogical enclave and it is high time someone exposed this scandalous practice. I refer to the monthly bulletins, one or two pages of total tripe! Now it's not quite so bad, and perhaps even understandable, to pay for postage to mail that sort of garbage to the locals, that is, persons who live within 100 miles of the society headquarters. Since most of what the bulletin features is news about the coming meeting of the group and the subject of the program, I'll concede that possibly sending that sort of enticing information might prod those nearby members into a little eager or even half-hearted participation. But when I live in California and the meetings are held in New Jersey, what in the sam hill benefit to me is it to read that Agnes FROBISHER brought cookies to the last gathering, or that they are taking sign-ups for a cleanup crew to perform on the coming Saturday at the county cemetery, or that there is a need for hostesses to volunteer at the historical museum every Wednesday. Good God, man, we're interested, but that's a heck of a commute!

Come to think of it, I'm not so sure that bulletins are even necessary for those members who live close to the home base of the society. Does anyone ever go to the meetings besides the officers? I guess they must, however, because the bulletins swear to it. But take me, for instance, I probably belong to at least a dozen of the blasted outfits, just so I can get my hands on the quarterlies with other people's ancestors in them. The plain truth, though, which recently dawned on me, is that in all the years I've been a multiple member, I had never wasted my time going to a meeting of any of them. Shucks, most of them are too far away, and the close ones would, just as sure as shooting, force me to sign one of their infernal lists of volunteers. So I steer clear. Then the other day, when I started writing this chapter, I realized that my anti-social conduct would surely result in short-changing the readers of this book (if there ever are any) and, quite frankly, perhaps even the societies themselves. I had a bounden duty, it seemed to me, to try to endure at least one meeting, or I could never call myself a specialist on the subject. If I could tackle it just once, then my conscience would be clear and I'd never have to go to another one! Well, as luck would have it, there was to be an all-day seminar held the very next weekend after I'd decided to martyr myself and make the sacrifice, and it was by one of the merry little bands to which I belonged. You can bet I looked forward to the day with a heightened sense of reluctance.

To further enhance this thrilling occasion, as it came to pass, it occurred smack-dab in the middle of a giant, record-breaking winter rainstorm! Just getting to the meeting place was going to take more than the usual amount of backbone since the whole area was battling storm warnings, travelers' advisories, power outages, already downed and about-to-come-down trees, flooded and closed roads and nearly hurricane-force winds. But, not being weak-hearted Nellies like they are back East, we Californians don't let a little erratic weather make up our minds for us about what we're going to do or not do, so my VW and I somehow wove and sputtered our way to the meeting.

From the appearance of the assembly room, the organizers were expecting quite a crowd, which didn't materialize, as it turned out. Since a number of area residents were busy being evacuated from their homes due to flooding, and other folks had been washed downstream or over cliffs, not too many of the remaining natives may have been particularly motivated to come to a meeting about dead relative collecting. Approximately 200 chairs had been set up, with sitters occupying about 25 of them. Of the 25, at least 15 were speakers, organizers or other head honchos. The whole shebang, as near as I could surmise, was aimed at educating poor confused beginners. But, when a show of hands was called for in order to identify any of those pathetic creatures, only four admitted it. I guess the rest of them, like myself, were either there for ulterior motives, had simply staggered in out of the incessant downpour or, seeing the coffee and doughnuts, perhaps mistook the place for an evacuation center.

After waiting a half-hour for the people who didn't ever show up, the first speaker recited a preview of coming attractions, which sounded about as spellbinding as cold spaghetti. Then she proceeded to pull the old signup sheet ruse. For those of you who are too naive to know what I'm referring to, that's when they pass around a clipboard, claiming that it is to be merely an historical accounting of those who attended the meeting. But after the seemingly innocent sheet has made the rounds and has been passed back up front, one of those devious tricksters who started it out in the first place will slyly insert a committee title at the head of the page. That's how they get volunteers! So, recognizing their subterfuge for what it was, I signed "Martha WASHINGTON". Let them figure that one out!

The second speaker was almost the only one in the room who didn't look like she'd just come in out of a deluge. It was not enough that she was more stylishly dressed than anyone there, but her platinum-blond hair (probably not her own) didn't have a strand askew and wasn't even damp. Maybe she had stayed there overnight because everything on her looked dry, not like the rest of us. Even her subject was dry, come to think of it. She passed out a hefty packet of things she said we *had to have* or we couldn't do it—be genealogists, that is. It jolly-well had to be her way or not at all! She would not compromise. She told us, as an example, that we were absolutely *not* to use yellow legal tablets (one of which I was visibly taking notes upon, and immediately felt all eyes were probably on me, accusingly). She staunchly declared that "to do research notes in the *proper* way," it had to be done on color-coded, 3-ring notebooks, or else! Pencils came next, followed by pens and erasers, the approved brand of each was demonstrated by being held high in the air by the dry lady to help us avoid being so stupid as to purchase the wrong kind, thereby killing all chances of becoming successful genealogists. Some members of the audience tried to engage in show-and-tell with their own pencils, pens and erasers but were quickly and without mercy silenced by the Absolute Authority up front, so as to protect the four uninitiated beginners from hearing things they shouldn't and, as a consequence, getting all confused about Materials.

Her presentation continued as she shared priceless information with us about Binder Clips, with an authorized

assistant holding up a sample so that, hopefully, we would be able to recognize it if we were ever confronted by one. She believed, for some strange reason, that the big, lumpy contraptions were superior to good-old reliable paper clips. (If you ever have occasion to open her file cabinets, I'll bet you'll see funny bulges and snagged paper all over the place, thanks to that particular hangup of hers.) Next in her talk came a subject which caused an immediate uproar amongst those of the audience who were not, by then, sound asleep. It was the exhilarating topic of how one should correctly cut paper. The complicated arguments of scissors versus a paper cutter and all the miniscule situations accompanying both procedures were debated with fiery support from one faction or the other. And, once they got heated up, there was a further clash over just how much to cut and where to stick it (with scotch tape, that is). One person, either hysterical or just trying to get her own opinion aired, shrieked out, "Don't punch holes in your paper and obliterate your notes!," which I thought was somewhat off the beaten path. Rightfully fearing she was on the verge of losing control, the speaker wisely, at that point, led us back to the subject of "correction tapes," which item proved to be safe because it was foreign to everybody there, so calm was restored.

After a steady 45 minutes of advertising about gadgets we were not supposed to be able to get along without (and, all the while, the four beginners and a few others taking frantic notes so they would have something to add to the rest of the junk in their briefcases), the lady plowed right into another controversial item—the Address Book. At that juncture, after she had indoctrinated us with her recommendation, she nearly got in a fist-fight with one of the men, who turned out to be a later speaker and an authority in his own right, because he had the gall to say he preferred a cheaper type than the one she was pitching. Well, you could immediately feel everyone tense up! The man held firm, however, and she finally backed off a tad, at least to the point of telling him that if he *had* to use the wrong kind, it was up to him, but she didn't want the beginners to start off on the wrong foot and purchase an address book which they would be sorry about later.

Still bristling a bit, the speaker moved on to her next Positive Necessity—briefcases, which she called "carry-alls" (she did have a southern accent, so maybe that was what was wrong with her). She just insisted we all had to have a "carry-all, attaché case, briefcase, tote bag, etc." to take with us whenever we did our research. Suddenly it came to me in a flash! *This* lady was the person who was probably responsible for creating so many researchers who fell into the designation on page 4 of this book, called the "BRIEFCASE MAGNET"!

As she was droning to a close, and after flipping through the countless mimeographed pages of "Must-Have Tools," which she had given each of us, I came to the conclusion that anyone who laid out all the money it would take to finance what seemed like a complete working inventory of a well-stocked office supply store (not even considering where a person was supposed to keep it all) would then be too broke to have anything left over to spend on research itself. But, to give her grudging credit, one thing I did learn from sitting through her speech was that I had just done five whole years' worth of record-keeping completely and totally all wrong!

The audience, by that time beginning to show signs of "hard chair paralysis," was not allowed to take a break (probably lest they not return), but was driven relentlessly onward by the immediate presentation of the next speaker, the man who had had the temerity to challenge Lady Bountiful of the Office Supplies. A few seconds into his talk, it became obvious that the poor soul was doing an excellent imitation of a character Don KNOTTS used to play in the movies, that of the petrified speech-maker. He hadn't displayed any of these tendencies of stage fright during his voluntary bout with the previous speaker, perhaps because he'd been sitting down in the warm, protective safety of the audience during that fracas. Now it was a different story. It must have taken true grit to stand up there in front of those twenty-odd people, shaking like a leaf. His subject was "Forms" (not anatomy forms—it wasn't *that* kind of a meeting), the type you can buy to pacify the needs of a firmly entrenched genealogy habit. Unfortunately, when an extremely nervous speaker supplements his prepared speech by holding up papers, pamphlets and other items, all quaking frantically, audience members are faced with a painful dilemma—where to look? Does one go eye-to-eye with the jittery subject himself, undoubtedly adding to his trepidation, or try to focus on whatever object is agitatedly waving in the breeze? Since the forms were almost unrecognizable at that speed, he could barely identify them himself. Luckily, he had pinned some of them to the wall before the meeting began and, as that assortment was well grounded, he shifted his attention to them, but, in doing so, brought on another problem. The sheets he had pinned up were not blank documents, as they probably should have been, but were covered with his own family research. This, now, was familiar ground and acted upon him like a life-preserver thrown to a drowning man. Shaking much less violently, he proudly launched into a prolonged account of minute details of his own early family, a subject of great interest to him but of no earthly use or interest to anyone else in the room. Finally, as some folks were already starting to get up and walk out, the second speaker, undoubtedly seeking revenge on him anyway, broke into his monotonous reverie in a loud voice, telling him to get back on the subject or sit down. Well, that reprimand revved up his shaking once again to high gear, but he soon decided the whole thing wasn't worth it and came to an abrupt halt.

Whoever programmed the meeting must have either been a sadist or blessed themselves with superhuman endurance, because we had been planted on those seats for over three hours with no relief, and doggoned if they didn't barge forward into the next presentation! Happily, the fourth speaker wasn't a disaster like the others, but, because she was such a good speaker and covered her subject so well, she contributed almost nothing for me to poke fun at. She spoke about how to successfully bug your older relatives for information. She stressed getting to those folks before they up and died on you and "took their information with them." One heartbreaking example in her own family, she said, was when she intended to go

visit her Aunt Mabel, with the intent of prying information out of the old girl, but Aunt Mabel pulled a fast one
and succumbed instead, "so they just missed her" (as if
Aunt Mabel were a train, waiting at the station). She also
advised cornering reluctant kinfolk (live ones, that is)
with a tape recorder, but doing it diplomatically so they
wouldn't pop you one or, worse still, clam up. She empha-
sized that you should also soft-pedal it when handling
bastards in the family. Whether you were interviewing one
direct or just asking about one, she didn't specify. She did
allude to the fact that some folks were very thin-skinned
and got embarrassed over almost any little aberration that
might cast aspersions (like the hanging of a family member, perhaps?). Now I always thought that sort of thing
rather livened up a family history, most of which tend to
be too dull anyway, but I may be in the minority.

There must have been a plot connected to the program
planning for this particular meeting, because the agenda
only provided a mere ten minutes right before lunch for
questions from the by-then paralyzed audience. Obviously,
they didn't want very many even from those who were still
awake. It turned out to be a blessing; there were only
two—one from a lady who wanted to do census searching
in 1870 and had no idea where her family was at that
time, and another from a man who was trying to trace a
rather flighty great-grandfather whose prime interest in
life was marrying various women and then moving on to
somewhere else, all without the benefit of a divorce court
(sounded like *my* grandfather, come to think of it). So
much for all the questions, which, by the way, got no
answers.

Finally, the meeting ground to a thankful lunchtime halt
and everyone bolted for the storm outside. Now I had
taken a sacred vow to sit through one whole meeting, as

you know, and I must hereby confess, I cheated! By the time I waded out to my VW, I was struck by the uncontrollable urge to keep going and to call it a day. Five or six more speakers were scheduled for the afternoon and, if they ran true to form, would easily provide me with an entire yellow legal tablet (not officially recommended) full of material, but I had run out of antacid pills and any remaining desire to be a human sacrifice, all at the same time. So if anyone reads this and somehow feels short-changed by my lack of staying power, they will just have to attend a meeting on their own to ferret out any additional tantalizing details of what they are all about.

If you decide, for reasons of your own, to take a rain-check on attending genealogical society meetings for awhile in favor of a preference to concentrate on your family research instead, doing what's in the next chapter should thrill you no end. All you need is a fairly reliable car, probably a husband or wife or friend or dog (in no particular designated priority) to accompany you, and a lot of free time. Oh, and *MONEY*. Only by doing it in a car across thousands of miles of countryside will you experience the true meaning of dead relative collecting.

The
Research Trip —
A Masochistic
Journey

If your spouse gets on your nerves at home, just think what spending 15 or 16 hours a day imprisoned in a car tooling across abominations like Nevada will do to your marriage! If they just didn't put those wide, boring states, such as Wyoming, Nebraska and Kansas, between you and Illinois, it would be a lot easier. But you can always cheer each other up (or perhaps become more deeply depressed) by talking about what a nightmare the same journey must have been for your ancestors going in the opposite direction behind an ox or something with no stereo or air-conditioning. That should put you right in the mood. What else is there to talk about through 1947 miles or more of nothing to look at but sagebrush, buttes and cornstalks (or whatever that endless stuff is they grow in Iowa)?

My strong recommendation about research trips is to try to get to your furthest desired location first, and preferably as fast as possible, before you get sick. I don't know how it is with you younger genealogists, but, if you are a little long in the tooth, I can just about guarantee that you'll suffer all kinds of physical ailments on a research trip. Unfortunately, it seems to be a certainty. Maybe it's the vibrations, or the water, or eating every night in a McDonald's to save money, I don't know, but the further you get from home the more frequent the rest-room stops are going to become. Indulging in a refreshing Kaopectate cocktail every hour or so might take care of some of your looser anxieties. I don't know what my husband takes, but he sleeps a lot, even clear through whole states on occasion. In fact, I sometimes have trouble getting him to wake up and pay for the gasoline. But if I can get a reasonable degree of consciousness out of him at courthouses or when it becomes his turn to drive, his otherwise constant hibernation beats having to carry on a conversation with him about the mechanical intricacies of farm machinery or one of his other favorite exciting topics. So I let him snooze all he wants.

If you are one of those kinky kind of individuals who won't travel unless you take your home with you (like a snail, so to speak) in the form of one of those obnoxious monsters some idiot has dubbed "recreational vehicles,"

those slow-as-molasses nuisances which magically appear in front of you to slow you down to a crawl and block your view on all winding, hilly two-lane roads, then you'd best skip this next part, which should only be of interest to us civilized, faster, non-recreational folks who stay in motels. Or, if you are simply rolling in dough and only allow yourself to be caught in a luxury motel, you might also pass over this section because you obviously need no help in picking out the joints acceptable to you. The same goes for you penny-pinchers who automatically head for the rockbottom bargain shanties or just hole up in a rest area and sleep in your car. The next bit of advice, you see, is primarily aimed at those of you who are willing to take a little chance now and then on lodging best classified as being at neither extreme and which might offer you some adventure for your money. Permit me to share a few examples.

In a county seat in southwestern Pennsylvania where everything appeared to be covered with black soot, we found a fascinating motor lodge on the outskirts of town. In the office was a barred teller-window with a mirror covering all the area behind the bars except for about three inches at the bottom, which looked like the top of a tiny counter. (We wondered if the mirror was the same type the police use in lineups, where you can look through it one way but not the other.) A disembodied voice said, "May I help you?" The entire business transaction was carried on back and forth in the space under the barred mirror with a person we never saw, except for her hands. As for the motel itself, it consisted of one long building of rooms with a wide parking driveway (a quick escape route, no doubt). The doorway entrance to the room we'd been assigned was a good two feet in the air, with no steps provided. I'd hate to think of the fate which would befall a patron with a short memory who might decide to step outside that room in the middle of the night. Inside there was one light in the bedroom, a bare bulb hanging third-degree style from the ceiling, and a matching light source in the dinky bathroom. The only other furniture besides the bed was one chair that must have been a reject from a salvage store. There was no phone or other accoutrements. Funny, that part of Pennsylvania seemed to attract very restless travelers, because all night long there were cars driving in and out, and a lot of giggling and female voices calling out goodbyes. Maybe they were showing movies? In the morning the only ones stirring were ladies sending young children off to school. Strange place!

In another county seat in western Missouri, somehow connected with Harry TRUMAN, were two motels, one on either side of the main road to town. Being motel connoisseurs at this point (it was our third research trip), we instantly identified and headed for the one recognizable as the least expensive. The sunken-in mattress and unyielding pillows were about par for the course, but the *pièce de résistance,* which remained in our memories a long time afterward, was the fact that the motel was situated right next-door to a pasture full of braying donkeys. What ambience!

By the way, one handy tip for saving money is that instead of aiming your nightly stop for what may seem to be the convenience of a big city, try to pick a spot in a small town near the big city. Except for Nevada, where there is no such thing anyway (they're *all* small towns in Nevada, even the big ones, a million miles from anywhere), the motel in the small town won't be as fancy, but it also won't siphon as much out of your pocketbook. Choosing this option qualifies you to participate in an exciting pastime. Have you ever tried mailing a series of postcards to friends and relatives from towns such as Pisgah, Iowa or Horace, Kansas, saying, "We're on our dream vacation—wish you were here!"? The only difficulty you might experience is in the selection of, or the lack of, postcards in some of those places, like I did in Albion, Nebraska and Oldtown, Maryland, where I was informed by store clerks that there wasn't too much of a demand. On another occasion we bought some spectacular postcards with "Miami" emblazoned all over them, and really impressed our friends back home, except for the discerning ones who took the time to read the full address and discover we were having a fling in Oklahoma, not Florida.

In some areas of the country you will simply find yourself at the mercy of whatever is available in the way of

motels. We once wanted to visit a certain Civil War battlefield in Kentucky, where Alan's grandfather had managed to reduce his customary number of legs by one,
thanks to a well-aimed Confederate Minié ball. We had
previously written, asking about recommended lodging.
The closest accommodations, we were told, were two in a
nearby small town. One was quite close to the railroad
tracks and was further enhanced by far too many unsavory
looking men hanging around, each of whom appeared as
if he might have just disembarked from a free ride in a
boxcar. We allowed as how we'd be lucky to make it
through the night alive and in possession of our meager
valuables if we registered at that seedy lodge, and our car
would probably be stripped in record time as well. So we
headed for the other one, praying it would at least be in a
classier neighborhood. Sadly, I don't think that poor little
burg had such a thing, as it was in no imminent danger of
being named the "Showplace of America." Instead, the
whole bailiwick looked like an excellent candidate for
Blight-of-the-Year Award. The second motel probably
dated to the 1920s or 1930s and may have been considered
pretty ritzy during that time period, sort of a U-shaped
Hollywood modern. Two men in bib-overalls and duck-
billed caps were sitting on kitchen chairs out in front of
the office, watching the cars go back and forth. An old
Ford truck was up on blocks in the yard, going nowhere.
Neither was the Hindu, or whatever he was, in a turban
and floor-length robe sitting beside it, taking in the sun.
In the spirit of adventure, we reluctantly registered.

Our room must have been endowed with very few
decorating changes since the long-ago day when the opening ceremonies ribbon was cut, and I truly believe the
present management employed only myopic cleaning
ladies or none at all. Perhaps it had been designated a

wildlife sanctuary or the housecleaning crew hated to exterminate any of God's creatures, because the bedroom, and the bathroom in particular, had more than the usual supply of very much alive and active spiders and awful crawly things that I guessed were cockroaches or some other less-than-desirable pet. Maybe they flourished in the humidity?

Another thing, we had trouble imagining what could possibly be occupying the room next to ours. A pickup truck backed right up to the door and a cowboy unloaded his saddle and a bale of hay and lugged them inside. Either they stole hay in those parts or his horse lived there. Kentuckians are pretty partial to their horses, we understand. The clientele were all fairly quiet that night (no loud talking or neighing), but perhaps that was because it wasn't Saturday night. Are you beginning to understand how many sacrifices we genealogists are forced to make in the pursuit of our glorious hobby?

Another bit of advice I offer freely is, "Never stay in Wyoming on a Saturday night!" Now Wyoming, in case you didn't know, is a land of grandeur, wide open spaces, and towns which are pretty far apart, but not far enough that the cowboys can't find them on a weekend and liven things up to a fever pitch. On the first day of a trip we used to like to drive from California straight through to Evanston, Wyoming, because there was a great steak restaurant in that town. But, after a nightmarish experience there one year, we are now content to stay in good old stodgy Salt Lake City instead. On the occasion we would best like to forget, we had put up in a different motel than our usual one (maybe that was the problem) and, instead of an elderly couple from Des Moines next-door, the manager had let the room to a bunch of local cowboys, very drunk local cowboys. More and more of them kept arriving and departing in screeching and dangerously weaving vehicles, from which they fell or staggered, barely able to stand up. There were loud yells and occasional vomiting noises coming from the adjoining room and then someone must have discovered a new game to play which seemed to consist of throwing each other or the furniture against the walls. We sleeplessly endured all this until about 2 A.M., hoping they would all pass out, but that was not to be. So we got up, gathered our suitcases and quietly left town. So never again, Evanston, you've had your chance and you flunked.

Now, I saved the best example of our ideal lodging place, one which fits in perfectly with our hobby, until last. It is the old Commercial Hotel in Osceola, Missouri, built in 1867 and operating ever since (at least I hope it is still going strong). And it has the convenience of being right across the street from the courthouse. When we first arrived at that location midday on a Sunday, we couldn't believe our good luck when we spotted a sign on the side of the building saying guests were welcome, so, sensing a wild adventure in the offing, we parked right in front of the old place and stepped through the front door into the past. The only trouble was that no one appeared to be there! We wandered around the totally deserted entry rooms till we came to the ornate parlor and found what seemed to be the only human on the whole ground floor. It was a very old lady, looking almost embalmed, rigidly ensconced in a straight-backed chair in the high-ceilinged room, staring straight ahead. We were not quite sure she was even alive until she finally spoke: "They're downstairs." Sure enough, when we found "downstairs", we also discovered what must have been a sizable portion of the Osceola population, feasting on what turned out to be the famous Chicken Dinner, which is considered an event of such magnitude as to rate honorable mention on the local road map. Everything stops for the Chicken Dinner, including the registration of hotel guests, mainly because the hotel desk clerk doubles as the waitress downstairs. Since we had gotten there too late to partake, she suggested we wait upstairs in the parlor until she got finished. The old lady had, by then, wandered off or died, and was no longer in occupancy, allowing my husband and me exclusive use of the picturesque old sitting room. I wouldn't have been the least surprised to see the ghost of Jesse JAMES or one of the YOUNGER brothers saunter through on their way to the bank (in fact, the YOUNGERs probably did before one of them was killed nearby). We imagined that the antique furnishings could have been part of the original hotel decorating scheme and most of them seemed sturdy enough to still be there far into the future, when our grandchildren might choose to visit the place with their own families, providing it was still in operation.

When the waitress finally returned and undertook the transformation to desk clerk behind the monstrous carved mahogany counter in the vestibule, she gave us the choice of a room with a bathroom all its very own (she proudly boasted that they had a few such rooms nowadays), or the usual bedroom-only where we would have to go down the hall and share a communal facility with the other hotel inhabitants. We decided, for once, that the sky would be the limit and we would splurge on first class. She asked, "Would $12 be OK?" Since $35 was about the cheapest going rate for which we had gotten lodging elsewhere that fall, we thought that being "big spenders" with deluxe accommodations in this ritzy hostelry was going to be just great! Our room, we soon learned, was upstairs on the south side, which put it three floors above the street. The stairway reminded us of the kind Mae WEST undulates down in the movies, and the hallway up there was wide enough to drive a stagecoach through, with solid old wood doors opening off it. The room itself must have originally been considered quite spacious and luxurious with its high, intricately-patterned ceiling and delicate wallpaper. To pacify present-day travelers who have come to expect that sort of thing, someone had plopped down a toilet, basin and bathtub in one corner of the huge square room, which must not have fit in too well with the existing decor, necessitating the rigging up of a six-foot high partition around them. While not technically accurate, it could now be called two rooms, or "Missouri Modern."

Once we had used the old-fashioned key to let ourselves in the door, we were both struck by qualms of nervous anxiety, wondering how we would ever get out of such a perfect firetrap in case a fire started. The fact that the structure had been standing for 115 years did little to reassure us, but we need not have worried because we soon saw that the management was already two steps ahead of us with their own well-prepared and practical safety plan. A card tacked to the inside of the door bore hand-writ, pencilled instructions: "In case of fire, use rope." Sure enough, coiled up under one of the two windows was a very long 1½-inch thick length of rope, knotted every two feet and fastened to the steam radiator (which would have probably also exited in case of fire, along with whoever used the rope). So our fire fears were soothed (somewhat).

In case you are wondering about the type of furnishings we encountered in such a relic of the past, they were just that, all of them. Each was a museum piece in its own right. The tall oak dresser tilted a bit toward the door, but that was its prerogative due to advanced age. And we discovered a mystery in one of the drawers—an old knife, stashed there by whom and for heaven knows what reason? Perhaps when you went down the rope, you were supposed to carry it with you, between your teeth? When you got in bed, you really got *in* it, because the mattress on the ancient iron bedstead had long ago given up the ghost of firmness and had pretty well caved in towards the center. Lighting fixtures in both the main room and the "annex" were like those in the Pennsylvania brothel or roadhouse or whatever it was, bare bulbs on the end of very long cords attached to the ceiling. And when you pulled the dangling chain to flush the commode, or ran water in the "bathroom," everyone in the hotel must have heard it because the travel route of the water was clearly audible all the way to the basement.

Being the Sabbath, there was no wild entertainment (or any other kind either) in town. I would hazard a guess that the Chicken Dinner was the solitary social event of the day, maybe even of the week. So we took a hike around the square, inspecting all the antiquated buildings, most of which, I imagine, were standing there in Grandfather's time. After we had made the Grand Tour, we sat on the front porch of the hotel, all alone, and I expect that was because the remainder of the town's citizens were recovering from chicken satiation. So it was left to the two of us to indulge in the frenzied excitement of monitoring the local traffic. Five cars and about an hour later we'd had our fill of that activity. Everything closes down on a Sunday in Osceola, so it was somewhat like being on the scene of a deserted western movie set and about as lively. By the way, the hotel did boast other guests, but the majority that we saw were almost the same age as the hotel and probably no longer desired much in the way of social excitement. Needless to say, it was quiet as a tomb that night, except for our own periodic outbursts of laughter prompted by our surroundings. Although the big front door remained unlocked, the desk clerk had long since departed and the quaint establishment may as well have been sitting in the middle of a ghost town. But it was a stay we will never forget. I hope every genealogical traveler can experience at least once (which will probably be enough) the thrill of staying in a Commercial Hotel of their own.

Now we'll get on to the other aspects of the research trip. Therefore, we will welcome back into the fold all you RV addicts and the others who skipped the subject of lodging, that is, if it is your habit to partake in the custom of eating. Come to think of it, I guess it might be premature to advise the RVers to pick up reading again. Don't they carry along their groceries, like kangaroos or squirrels or something, and go on forcing their womenfolk to cook like they were not even on a vacation? So you recreationals can bug off!

Eating places come in two varieties, expensive and fast-food. How does the thought of a Big Mac and a chocolate milkshake every night for three weeks grab you? I thought so, but think of the money you'd save. And you could tote along fruit and nuts in your car to take care of breakfast and lunch. Your doctor at home would probably be pleased no end at that arrangement, envisioning all sorts of neat health problems upon your return, if not sooner. I will agree that the above recommendation is not for everyone, but it is about the bare-bones minimum for stretching your proposed food budget on a trip. If you are over-endowed with a fat bank account and want to create the image of being known as a gourmet, you might very well become nauseated at this suggestion, as you will surely dine only in four-star ptomaine palaces, so you can dress for dinner. If you are already dressed, from a side trip to the local cemetery, you will look out of place in a really froufrou bistro, where they don't care to entertain too many red-eyed patrons in rain slickers and knee-boots in the middle of July.

Immersed in the genealogy hobby, your travels could very well take you to numerous parts of the United States, and perhaps to foreign countries. Unless you are an old stick-in-the-mud about what you eat and will only consent to ingesting such items as you can easily recognize, fixed the way your dear old mother used to cook them, you should on occasion take a big wild chance and expose yourself to some of the weird treats people in other parts of the country think of as edible. To give you one example, we pulled into a certain county seat out in the hinterlands in mid-Missouri one evening about dinnertime. The teeming municipality had one sole business street approximately two blocks long, which sported two cafes, so we actually had a choice. The first one only had one customer in it, which didn't advertise well for its cuisine. The other was busily serving at least forty hungry souls in what appeared to be a converted department store or bus terminal. For obvious reasons, we chose the latter and drew some scrutiny when we walked in, it being after the tourist season and we being the only strangers in town. We stood out immediately because we were too stupid to know whether to wait for a hostess (they didn't have one of those, nor probably know what they were) or just go sit at a free table. One of the diners called out directions. The interior of the barn-like eating-house had an interesting atmosphere. The floor was buckled in spots and the worn carpet went along with the act by humping up accordingly, making walking gracefully to one's table slightly hazardous. What looked like a giant air-conditioning unit, or some such piece of machinery, hung precariously from the bowed ceiling, threatening to fall free any minute and squash the customer who was foolish enough to sit beneath it. Formica tables of various styles and sizes were scattered informally hither and yon around the room. The specialty of the house turned out to be catfish! Yuk, we thought! But, famished and not wanting to offend the waitress and the other locals who were greedily shoveling it in, we decided to give it a try. While the restaurant will probably never be featured in *Bon Appétit,* the meal wasn't *too* bad and we weren't sorry we took a chance.

By the way, while we're on the subject of Missouri and its peculiar delectables, what in the world gave them the audacity to try to produce their own wine? Now their Concord grapes are delicious, I'll concede them that. We never miss a chance to purchase those while driving through southern Missouri. If you have a big appetite and buy enough of them, you can spit seeds out the window all the way to Virginia, if your grape supply doesn't rot on you first. But, as a native-born Californian, which equates to being a natural-born wino (is that the proper term for wine expert?), I couldn't believe my eyes when I saw the signs along the highway, near one of our regular grape stands, touting local wine and wineries. I suppose having grapes gave them the idea. If you ever want to play a joke on your friends in California (or in any of the other 49 states, for that matter), for Christmas give them a bottle of Missouri wine, the *vin ordinaire* of the wine-tasting world. But what can you expect when all they have to enrich their vines is mule manure?

As you take care of your own body while you are on a genealogical trip, by sampling grapes and wine in Missouri, scrod in Boston, grits in the south, and God-knows-what in Texas, so will it be necessary to feed and pamper

your automobile or it will break down on you when you least expect it. I do believe a car's designers planned the bloody varmint to be nearly 75% reliable all year long while performing its daily duties, but take it on a research trip and look out! And, in the most devious manner, it picks and chooses the very worst possible time to conk out. We had a brand new VW Rabbit (perhaps that alone showed a certain lack of good judgment?) simply go dead as a doornail the furthest back we could drive in Bryce Canyon, Utah (we were cheating a little on the research and trying to do some sight-seeing). Another time the same irresponsible vehicle began leaking gas in the middle of western Kansas (exactly half-way between either of the major east-west highways), continued on through eastern Colorado, and it was only by the skin of its radiator that it was able to limp into the fix-it place in Colorado Springs, one of our favorite repair garages, among many. You do know, of course, that you can expect to be on a first-name basis with mechanics all across America if you persist in taking research trips.

In fairness to the car, it is not always to blame. On more than one occasion, in a mad frenzy to get the window opened or closed, I did it so violently that the window handle remained in my hand after I had exited the vehicle, causing a search for a parts shop. On another occasion, my husband, probably asleep at the time because he claimed it was dark, checked the oil and forgot to put the oil cap back on. It is surprising how far oil can fly, unhindered. And, in that particular case, we learned that unless you are driving a Ford or a Chevy, in the rural area of southwestern Ohio, you had better count on a *long* drive to a parts store. VWs and their ilk are totally foreign there! Maybe it's not a bad idea to stuff extra oil caps, a little baling wire and a repair manual in your briefcase with your family charts before you leave home.

Now it isn't *de rigueur* to spend every daylight hour of your genealogical research trip doing research. On occasion you are permitted to reward yourself with fun and games. However, your little side-amusements, if they are to truly count as kosher to genealogy, should reflect some phase of living, or dying, in the past. By this time you are probably fed up to the gills with examples, but you will just have to sit still for some more.

Early one drizzly September morning, 123 years to the month after the battle took place, my husband and I parked near one of the battlefield sites in the Chickamauga and Chattanooga National Military Park in Georgia. The scene was a ghostly hill perched above the river, with nothing to offer but a foggy mist, old iron cannons, historical monuments and dripping trees. We were the only live beings in sight the entire time we were there that particular morning, and we let our imaginations run rampant while our camera ran out of film. So infused by this experience were we with the immediate and overpowering desire to walk around on other pieces of real estate where thousands of people had been slaughtered, that we visited all the battlefields we could find where our various earlier family members had not ducked successfully. The ones we liked best were those least spoiled by modernized gadgets. Somehow it is hard to get into the spirit and be able to visualize a bloody battle in a bucolic green pastoral setting by pressing a button on a post and listening to a recorded voice telling about it. Someone should take one of those trusty cannons and blow every last talking post to kingdom come! But, enough of that. If you are a cannon freak or get your kicks out of reading inscriptions on upright hunks of granite, or if you just dig quiet spots which were once scenes of terrible violence and bloodshed, you might get thoroughly whipped up by visiting the Civil War battlegrounds.

Once you become an experienced genealogist who has succeeded in finding and translating old family land records and matching them to today's plat maps, then you are not going to rest easy until you see for yourself the exact section or piece of land where your ancestors built their log cabins or whatever. This is an entirely understandable trait, like a swallow returning to Capistrano (except *they* don't need maps). Now, when it comes to the actual ancestral building, you will have to understand and come to grips with the fact that not too many of them erected in the 1700s and early 1800s are still standing today, so be prepared for probable disappointment on that score. All that was left of my grandfather's sod hut on his homestead site in Nebraska was nothing. Two corn cribs marked the spot where it may have been built, and a cow stood in the middle of the dirt section road, looking mildly curious, but that was it! Of course, being a true and rabid genealogist, I promptly trespassed on the land (I couldn't see anyone anywhere to ask permission of, except the cow) and, as is our hobbyist's sacred duty, scooped up a couple of rocks to take home. As you can imagine, every time my eyes light fondly upon those rocks, I relive the thrill of gazing on that Nebraska pasture where my family almost starved to death.

One example of an early structure which was still standing in all its questionable glory since 1842, was doing so mainly because the locals were scared stiff of going near it. Not too many of you will be lucky enough to discover a family haunted house! It helps if your lineage, like mine, is peppered with horse thieves and murderers who spiced up their daily activities with bloody feuds and shoot-'em-ups conducted all over the countryside, and quite often from their actual living quarters themselves. Spill enough blood on the premises, I always say, and your house will stand a jolly-good chance of being avoided by folks, then and later. The one in our family, long ago dubbed "Fort Underwood" by various law officers who refused to go near it, was in eastern Kentucky, a land where the inhabitants had a lot of free time in which to take offense at things and then proceed to help their case along with the aid of a Winchester. It certainly *was* a clear, concise way to settle an argument, you will have to agree, providing you drew first, or were well hidden behind a big tree.

But I digress. Back to our visit to the haunted house. I had heard the old stories of the final massacre and murder there of my brave family members by a band of despicable, yellow-bellied cowards (you can tell I'm trying hard to remain neutral) who snuck up and, hiding behind trees as was generally their practice, bushwhacked one of my law-abiding relatives outside the house, after which they forced their way indoors past the terrified womenfolk and cold-bloodedly murdered the man's unarmed and previously wounded aged father in his bed. All for no reason, of course, because everyone knew my family was the embodiment of peacefulness in the community. (The story became part of a recent bicentennial pageant in a nearby town—how many families can boast about something like that!)

I had also heard that Kentuckians are known for their long memories, like elephants. Once they get an idea strong enough, they don't let go of it too quickly. Even though it was 104 years after that last shooting at the old house, not counting those in the neighborhood in 1903 and 1927 and others, I guess, too numerous to mention, involving my family members, I was a little nervous that the word would get out that there was an UNDERWOOD back in town. Any of you who have uncovered ancient feuds in your lineage won't find any advice in the average genealogical "how-to" book about how you should prepare yourself for a visit back to where the guns had blazed. The local telephone book showed way too many names of descendants of those on the other side in the biggest feud, indicating that my family's aim wasn't as good as it should have been or they hadn't done a very thorough job. I had no way of knowing, of course, if they still bore a grudge and went around armed. After all, there were quite a lot of big trees to conceal themselves behind. Poor defenseless me, all I had in the world to defend myself with were my knitting needles and a loaded 22 in the glove compartment, so I was at a disadvantage. (By the way, the only difference between me and all those ancestors who were charged with carrying a concealed weapon was that they got caught at it! One must maintain family tradition!)

The college professor who now owned "Fort Underwood" was the one who confirmed tales of the old place being haunted. His folks had tried living in the house, had covered most of the blood and bullet holes with wallpaper, and had met up more than once with the specter of "Old George" on his ghostly patrol. At first I thought he was putting me on, but because of what happened there that day, I will never scoff at the possibility of anything the locals might see or experience at that place.

As the professor, Alan and I climbed down some stone steps to the level of the old building, almost totally concealed in a thick grove of trees (designed for a modern-day ambush, I wondered?), two gangling teenage boys materialized from nowhere. I recognized their surnames as distant kin, as, I later learned, were most of those who lived in that hollow. They had seen the California car and hoped its occupants were headed for the old house. With good luck, they allowed as how they might get a chance to see the insides of a structure they had lived near and been scared about their whole lives but hadn't ventured this close to, even in broad daylight, due to the "haunts." Well, I felt safe, I told them, because both of my great-grandparents had been UNDERWOODs, so I didn't consider myself a threat to "Old George," my great-grandfather's brother. But now I wonder if there were also ghosts hanging around of some of those on the other side of that old feud, who may not have been so friendly? Because, while we were in the room where "Old George" and his son were said to have breathed their last, I suddenly felt something strange on the inside of my left arm and, looking down, was startled to see that it was blood! A long scratch had appeared, freely bleeding, yet I'd had no conscious knowledge of what had caused it, I swear, and don't to this day. Had I perhaps come in contact with a sharp paw-paw branch outside and not even been aware of it? Or had I joined the ranks of other family members whose blood was lost in that place?

The other hard-to-explain item that happened there that day was not evident until we returned home and developed the pictures we had taken on that occasion. In one particular outside shot of the old home, everyone there that day had either been in the snapshot or taking it, and the position of each was well established. In the picture there are shadows on the old house, all the same darkness but one, and that one appears to be the lighter, grey shadow of a man, wearing an old-fashioned tall hat. None of us was standing where we could have made that shadow and no one was wearing a hat of that kind. Did "Old George" go along with us that day? I hope so.

If you can't come up with a haunted house in your past and scare up the ghost in residence, there are other avenues you can pursue to try to duplicate how things must have been in the daily lives of your ancestors. We tried to every chance we got. Once we experienced the thrill of silently gliding down a river in the Ozarks, just the two of us, in a rented canoe. True, it was fiberglas, not birchbark, but nowadays you have to take what is available. We also experienced the thrill of leaning too far to the left to avoid getting our skulls fractured on a swiftly approaching overhanging tree. It's called tipping over. I'm sure our forefathers went under the same as we did, frantically grabbing for their overturned canoes also and trying not to lose too many possessions and their lives in the swift current. But *they* probably didn't wind up with a non-waterproof 35-millimeter camera becoming fully submerged. Although perhaps in their case it may have been their muskets or some other much more necessary gadget which may have become inoperable thanks to the drenching.

In another attempt to "get in sync" with our forebears, on our many research trips we always asked relatives we visited for any family recipes which may have been handed down from earlier times in the various branches. More than one recipe, we discovered, was for soap! Have you ever tried to make your own soap like your great-grandmother had to do? We had to wait till we returned home, of course, but I can proudly say I did! The results were disastrous! I don't know what went wrong but something surely did because the finished product ate its way clear through my husband's sturdy two-inch solid workbench. If those soap recipes were correct, our predecessors must have had more than their share of dermatology problems!

I hope I've been able to give you a little prod toward considering a faraway adventure of your own. If you are either just beginning in genealogy, or have up to now confined your research to where you can travel easily from home base, believe me, a whole world of excitement awaits you in strange exotic places like Iowa and North Dakota. All you have to do is gas up and get going! For those of you who haven't saved up enough to finance your trip yet, or whose ancestors stayed in the same boring place they chose when they first got off the boat and where you, yourself, now live, or for those of you who have already gone on a trip, returned, and are still madly into genealogy in spite of everything, the highlight of your daily life (except Sundays and holidays) has got to be the arrival of your mailman!

You Will Have
an Affair With
Your Mailman

Most people like to receive mail. The genealogist goes absolutely berserk about receiving mail! Ask my mailman. I know he thinks I lie in wait for him. My eyesight is not so great anymore (too many hours spent perusing old records and darkened, out-of-focus census film), but my hearing is still good enough to pick up the distinctive rattling sound of the mail truck at least a half mile away. Believe you me, everything stops for the mail truck! People talking to me on the phone at the time get instantly hung up on. Visitors in our house are left staring at my empty chair as I make a wild grab for my jacket (in cold weather only, of course) and disappear out the door. God forbid that I should be cooking or in the bathroom because the mail simply takes priority over all else.

Our postal boxes in the rural area where we live are in a cluster "down the road a piece," as an old fruit picker I knew used to say. Our regular mailman has, I dare say, become used to the sight of a purple-jacketed overweight old broad charging down the hill toward him like a brightly colored water-buffalo on the rampage. Most days he barely has time to stuff the last of the announcements about the millions of dollars we've just won in some idiotic sweepstakes and the far-too-frequent taxpayer-paid-for brag-sheet by Senator Alan CRANSTON portraying the stupendous job he thinks he's doing in Washington, D.C. into the mailbox before I snatch them out again in a desperate search for something worthwhile, namely genealogical. On my better days, with an extra burst of speed, I can actually beat the mailman to the mailbox and on those occasions I feel it is in better taste to try to conceal myself, as best I can, behind the bushes, until he has performed his official duties, at which time it is considered fair game to pounce out.

I share the above information with you who are newly initiated into the hobby of genealogy so that when the inevitable symptoms of "Mail Mania" strike you (which can happen fairly quickly), you will recognize it as a not uncommon side effect and realize there is no need to take tranquilizers for the condition.

Incoming genealogical mail can roughly be divided into two categories—stuff from human beings and stuff from institutions (government, not mental). Obviously, you won't get any from the latter without a little effort and a lot of money on your part. But who besides a genealogist bursts forth into song when they discover a death certificate in their mailbox? Such an exciting document can be the highlight of your whole week! The average mailman will probably guess that you are not operating a numbers racket out of your residence, as he may have first suspected, when you suddenly start receiving more mail than anyone else in your neighborhood. The clue which helps him figure it out is when he begins to notice that most of the envelopes he brings you bear the return address of courthouses from many different parts of the United States. Then, if your mailman is brighter than most postal employees tend to be, he will either assume you are in a peck of legal trouble all over the country, or that you are into genealogy.

Sometimes the weird type of communications coming your way will impress your carrier no end and, as a result, you will gain new status and respect in his eyes. About a year ago when our regular mailman went on vacation his duties were covered by a fellow who drove, looked and talked like an illegal alien from Mexico. About that time I received a couple of letters from a family member who, at the time, happened to be the United States Ambassador to Mexico. The envelopes were clearly marked with his title and return address in gold lettering. On the first occasion the substitute mailman, realizing that he was the bearer of Something Important From The Homeland, drove his truck clear up the road right into our yard and was in the process of dismounting to come to our door, when I leaped out at him in my standard fashion. There really wasn't any excuse for his unusual, extra service, mind you, because the Ambassador's letter was not marked "Special Delivery," nor was anything else in my pile of mail. But he handed it over like he was delivering a missive from El Presidente. Then he formally introduced himself and started telling me some kind of story. As near as I could understand, not speaking Spanish very well, it was about his family, I think. From that day forward till the regular carrier returned, Ramon (he said I was to call him by his first name) delivered my mail right to my door and made a formal little bow when he handed it over. He probably thought he had made a "Connection."

It's surprising what a huge amount of genealogical research you can do without ever leaving your home, thanks to the U.S. Postal Service. This should come as welcome news to genealogists who become temporarily homebound due to being stripped of their driver's license for driving home from the research center in what that cranky officer of the law mistakenly declared was a drunken stupor (when *you* know, of course, that it was plain and simple projector fatigue, nothing more). You might also find yourself stuck at home if a live older relative living with you and doing worse than you are suddenly needs your constant care, or if you have a new litter of puppies in the house, or if you live in one of those strange parts of the country subjected to peculiar weather which dictates your movements, or for any number of other annoying reasons. Remember, so long as you maintain a supply of envelopes, stamps and writing paper, you're in business.

Now for those of you who are novices at the fine art of letter writing, having previously confined your postal efforts to perhaps twice-a-year obligation thank-you notes to relatives you do not like, for Christmas and birthday gifts you didn't want and couldn't use, you may easily start your genealogical letter writing campaign under the delusion that for every letter you write, one will come back to you in return. Foolish supposition! Ask any experienced genealogist. If we get one back for every five we send out we are deliriously happy. The consequences of your mailed appeals to individuals can be generally classed into the following three types:

1. The prompt or relatively prompt answer with no further goosing by you needed. A beginner foolishly dreams, and somehow expects, that everyone contacted will miraculously fall into this classification, that the recipient will be so thrilled to receive a request for information that he or she will promptly stop all their other daily duties and responsibilities, sit down immediately and neatly type pages and pages of old Bible records and other official, proven documentation that they just happen to possess, all about the intimate details of their family, just because a total stranger, somehow related to them, asks. Quite frankly, I can only vaguely imagine what happens at the other end when an initial genealogical appeal arrives at the house of a non-genealogist who is not expecting anything of the sort, but I can assure you it rarely turns out as above. I suspect that some recipients might look upon the suspicious letter as a plot by the Communists or the I.R.S., or guess the nosy letter writer next plans to hit them up for a loan, drop in for a visit (heaven forbid!), or be bothering them out of the blue for some other dark, ulterior motive, because some of them *never* answer. And you know for a fact that they haven't deliberately thwarted you by dying because you always put your return address on the envelope and the letter didn't return. The truth you

will have to face is that the letter receiver, sad to say, may not give a hoot about the family history, may have a deep, abiding hatred for all relatives he or she has ever run across, or may have inherited all the worst of your family's mental problems and not be up to *any* writing, except on the walls of the room in which they are being kept.

2. The person who will finally send information six months or more later, providing you hound them relentlessly from about a month after your first inquiry to them has failed to produce any results. Remember, a dedicated genealogist will *never* give up. I once spent a small fortune in postage stamps and long distance telephone calls to a sluggish lady back East, listening patiently to every cockamamie excuse she could concoct for why she wasn't complying as yet to my request. I think I eventually just plain wore her out. She undoubtedly gathered up the data and sent it in self-defense, to put a stop to my bothersome, nagging phone calls and letters. You can invent a variety of handy reasons for follow-up telephone or mail coaxing, i.e. that you are just checking up to see if your previous letter arrived safely, mail delivery being as uncertain as it is, that you wondered if they had any questions about what you sent, did they need more postage stamps in order to send their records or extra money to run the copying machine, and so forth. . . . If you ride them with a tight enough rein, many of the seemingly reluctant procrastinators will finally realize that it will waste less of their time if they give up and send you what you have been badgering them for, than to continue to put up with you making their life miserable with your incessant pleading. So hang in there, fellow genealogists, and pester, pester, pester!

3. Those !@#$%¢&*()+ people you never hear from again, *ever*! The hardest thing to figure out about this maddening category is that it even includes persons

you initially think of as "easy marks" or "sure bets." By
that I mean folks on whom you have squandered sums of
money by telephoning them long distance, based on a
theory by some expert (or is it that constant advertising
barrage by AT&T?) that personal contact by telephone
(preferably through AT&T) pays off in results. In most
cases they sound warm, friendly and cooperative on the
phone and you feel certain that each one will answer,
mainly because these deceptive souls put on a pretty good
act of being very interested in the family history and your
whole project as you've described it to them. (Could it be
that they are just humoring you like one does a violent or
insane person?) But they give you their sacred oath that
they have stacks of old records, information and ancestral
pictures all ready to send, which they promise to do, causing you to begin slathering at the mouth in eager anticipation before you have even hung up the receiver, only to
find that they never keep their promise. And to further
frustrate you, they never live close enough, unfortunately,
so that you could hop in your car and drive to their place
and arm-wrestle them out of their bloody records. Forevermore you are haunted by the driving suspicion that
their elusive information, and theirs alone, contains all the
most important missing clues for which you have been
unsuccessfully searching for years, clues which would
solve all the still-unsolved mysteries in your family history.
It's enough to drive a genealogist barmy!

In order to avoid having all your letter receivers fall
assuredly into the last aggravating classification, you will
have to work a minor miracle and somehow come up with
a style and contents which will turn off as few people as
possible and give you at least a fighting chance of receiving an answer now and then. Your wild uncurbed genealogical enthusiasm can sometimes be your own worst

enemy, however, if it comes out the wrong way in a letter. The most maddening example I can recall personally involved one of our family researchers who, as it happens, is a successful business administrator in a collection agency in private life and has become accustomed to sending out strongly worded ultimatums and getting results from them. Well, he decided, all on his own, how he thought we might get more information for our family history and promptly assembled a list made up of relatives none of us had yet had the chance to contact and also those who had previously been approached but who hadn't responded. He composed what he thought was a jim dandy motivational letter and sent Xeroxed copies of it, with no return envelopes, to all of them. After he had done all this, he proudly informed all other family researchers of his project and enclosed a copy of the form-letter he had sent. It took me awhile to get over the urge to scream, cry and utter unladylike phrases, once I'd seen his letter, because it was obvious that not only would such an abominable genealogical collection caveat never result in an answer, unless it was an angry one, but would probably forever stifle any future attempts by the rest of us to expect any cooperation from those same potential sources. The problem with his letter was that too many years of contacting dead-beats in a determined effort to extract money from same had rubbed off on this particular researcher and greatly influenced his writing style. His letter sounded like a combination apology for embarrassing the family and a direct threat to answer, or else. Now a threatening letter is bad enough, but when it is not even a personal letter but a Xeroxed threatening letter, it would be headed right for the garbage can in most, if not all, places where it was received, of that I had no doubt.

So, what about the composition of the letters them-

selves, you ask? In the nearly six years I've been sending out postal appeals, trying to goad individuals into action, I have found the most effective ones are best compared to Sally RAND instead of to present-day nude dancers. "Give them a little, but not too much, so they will have to write to get more" is a good motto. Tease them with a fan of partial family details only, all the while hinting that you have file cabinets full of more fascinating information and that the incoming mail has just brought you a windfall of family secrets which you haven't had time to sort through as yet, but will gladly share after you've heard from them. Stress that you would have sent them more, but need their records and information first in order to know exactly which juicy items to pick out and send.

When I was a trusting, naive beginner, I made the stupid mistake, on an initial contact, of enclosing a hand-typed family chart showing the direct family line, as I had it at the time, all the way back from whichever person I was contacting. Well, some of the ungrateful wretches simply kept my overly generous offering (or at least I suppose they did) and never even wrote back a thank-you letter for it, nor did my subsequent efforts to shame them into communicating produce any results. Why should they, when you think about it, when I had already given them all they probably ever cared to know and more than enough to get them started on their own research if they were so inclined or were already working on their family history.

Now I don't know your reaction to receiving a form-letter, but they turn me right off. Xeroxed family charts and records are great, but Xeroxed letters are fit for only one container. When a stranger asks me to take my time to read their request and then use further time to sit down and type up a bunch of information and mail it to them (frequently using my own postage, to boot), then the very least they can do is to freshly type or hand-write their infernal form-letter so that it doesn't look like one. One of these days I might just compose my own form-letter answer to all form-letters, which you can bet will be at least 98% antagonistic, but, seeing as how it would still cost me a postage stamp to get revenge, I don't know if it would be worth it.

Almost all genealogical "how-to" books waste their time on the composition of request letters, like as if there is some kind of magic form and style which is guaranteed to bring results. I don't know what percentage of research-ers follow this well-meaning advice but I know some of them ignore it completely. Three years ago I received a perfect example of what the "how-to" books would call "The Worst Way to Write an Introductory Letter." It was from a lady in Indiana (maybe all they teach them back there is how to play basketball, not how to write successful letters), so I made allowances. The entire body of the letter didn't take up half a page. She briefly introduced herself and one ancestor born in 1840. She didn't include any other information to bribe or tempt me, nor offer to share anything she might have at a later date, but displayed what I considered to be a colossal nerve by asking for all I had on that particular family branch and, to further compound her outlandish behavior, didn't even accompany her brash demands by an SASE! Horrors! Top recognized genealogical lecturers would become incensed at this type of letter, which they would claim is most often wadded up and used, together with kindling, to help start fires in woodburning stoves, and they would probably be right. But I decided to answer that particular letter, I don't know why, perhaps only because the mail had been sparse that week and I had a little spare time. Well, that seemingly brusque note, as it turned out, came from one of the most thorough, diligent family researchers I've ever "met," who has since become one of my closest and dearest friends. I've never asked her, by the way, what her rate of return mail is from her initial requests, using that kind of frowned-upon approach, but just think what it would be if she followed the "rules"!

My Indiana friend was not the only person guilty of accosting me with a literary burr of this sort. On a few other occasions I have also opened envelopes containing brief requests that I send "all the information you have" on our family, with nothing offered in return. One such demand arrived when I was right in the middle of typing the final publisher's copy of the manuscript of my 718-page family history. Needless to say, my immediate and highly vocal outburst was not even printable. After I had simmered down and stopped frothing at the mouth, I lashed out with a huffy little note to the wretched cur, which probably did no more than convince him that I was suffering from hot flashes or some other such disorder. But I do feel that even if your devious purpose is to pry all the information you can out of a potential source (which is admittedly the intent of most of us genealogists), without giving anything in return (which is only the selfish practice of a very few), for heaven's sake, disguise your deviousness with a little diplomacy.

Once you manage some semblance of control over your own outgoing communications, what can you then expect in return? Well, if you initiate even a reasonable effort at contacting folks, your postal delivery or trip to your post office box should turn into a daily frenzy of fever-pitched excitement. Anything that isn't immediately identified as a bill, mail-order catalog, political advertisement, or other piece of annoying junk-mail may wind up being SOMETHING SENSATIONAL! (At least that will be the feeling you will likely have every day, until you open each item.) Envelopes bearing the return address of the National Archives, a courthouse or library will either lift you to the heights or send you into a fit of despair, depending on whether they contain a copy of the record you've requested or a disappointing form-letter saying they don't have/won't look for the record you are positive they are deliberately concealing back there someplace.

When it comes to personal letters, you had best be prepared for some you will barely be able to read. Accordingly, it will soon be apparent that not everyone is blessed with a typewriter or decipherable handwriting, but I guess you should be grateful that they communicated at all. Eventually, with a magnifying glass and help from others, you might even be able to figure out the information they have sent or what it is they might be asking you to do.

While we are on the subject of problem letters, and at the risk of touching on a delicate subject, I feel I must warn you, especially those of you who are younger and still in your right mind, that you will almost certainly receive some letters from us older folk which will forevermore remain a puzzle. As you know, certain people, as they get older, begin going through their days operating on fewer and fewer cylinders. If you are a long-time genealogist and this happens to you, take it from me, it won't put too much of a crimp in your usual activities and you will generally continue bravely, though not always rationally, with your precious hobby, both with increasingly disjointed research and equally disjointed letter writing. We "mature" genealogists sometimes forget if we have answered letters and wind up doing so twice or not at all, can't seem to remember what we have written to whom about what, send for the same records more than once, and lose mail. If I concentrate really well, thanks to my bifocals, I can confine my typing to reasonable margins, all within the outer perimeters of the paper on which I'm writing. Others, however, with even worse eyesight, I guess, are not always so lucky and their sentences wander off the page with regularity, further obscuring the meaning of what is quite often a rather confused letter at best, even if it were all written within bounds. We sometimes choose to go on writing to you younger genealogists long after we have made an attempt to answer your initial request for information because most of our own dear friends are now dead and so are not writing nearly as often as they once did. We write, you see, in the hope of getting a letter in return. It is not very often, especially as we get older, that we can rejoice in the happy feeling that we can be of some value to someone once more merely for the information we can impart. So, when you get a letter that is even stranger than usual, try to figure it out if you can, and do send an answer. Remember that in some folks' opinion all genealogists are slightly unhinged anyway, and only the degree of unhingement is debatable.

By the very nature of the hobby of genealogy, you probably won't get too many really angry letters, unless you write to someone who was known never to have married and ask for all the details of his or her illegitimate children, or make some other indelicate blunder when writing to a potential source of information. I have only received two angry letters so far, although that figure could climb once this book is out. One thoroughly ticked-off correspondent was under the mistaken impression that I was working in close collaboration with the collection agency family researcher, previously mentioned, who sent out those infuriating form-letters and therefore saw it as her bounden duty to threaten us both with a lawsuit or vague mayhem of some unspecified nature.

Another infuriated female who sounded Righteous and Pure as the Driven Snow and had taken enough umbrage to choke a horse at a promotional letter I wrote to try to sell my family history book, really let fly. What she was absolutely livid about was that I had mentioned including a section in the book about various family members who had gotten in trouble with the law for appropriating a goodly number of large, four-legged animals of the equine persuasion without benefit of money changing hands, those who were a little too casual in the use of loaded guns around people who irritated them, and others who could be classed on occasion as kicking up their heels in what might be looked upon as anti-social behavior. The incensed woman who, by the way, was not even a blood relative, merely a lowly in-law, having married into the family, got all hot under the collar and penned two pages of vitriolic wrath at me for daring to include anything negative about my own kinfolk and then turn around and publish same for the whole world to read. She predicted that the younger, innocent members of our family would, after reading my scandalous accounts of certain relatives, then and there forsake an honorable life and run completely amok with sin and depravity at least and maybe even criminal acts of their own. (Here I thought I'd just written a fairly boring family history and it was going to do all that, WOW!) Before she finally ran out of invective, she said she hoped one day someone would find out something about my family and publish it (?). Since it *was* my family I had written about, I was rather puzzled as to her meaning on that point, but her anger may have put her in such a highly excitable state that she'd lost track somewhat. She suggested that I should have deleted all the family criminal records, never collected them in the first place and, instead, made up nice heroic stories of some sort about each of what I referred to as "black sheep" so that the young folks would be inspired. Frankly, I don't know just how inspired young people would remain when they discovered, as they invariably would, that a person had been lying to them, as she was recommending that I do. This ruffled lady was, of course, reacting to my letter, not my book, which she hadn't seen as it had not yet even been published. I had tried my doggondest to compose as stimulating a letter as possible to pique people's interest in the book and promote sales, but I guess I sure over-piqued hers.

Now, as even a poor, simple genealogical beginner can probably fathom, in order to indulge successfully in your exciting chosen hobby of collecting dead relatives, you will almost surely have to write to live ones. There is no escaping it! And once you have taken that risky step, my friend, there's no telling what you have let yourself in for. While it is all well and good to call them "Cousin", send them Christmas cards, phone them now and then, and maybe even take such liberty as to conclude your letters with the closing, "Love", have you ever seriously thought what all this unchecked postal and long-distance camaraderie might lead to? Have you? Well, it just might prompt some of these strangers to take the Ultimate Step! Yes, perish the thought, they might be struck by the uncontrollable urge to MAKE PERSONAL CONTACT *IN PERSON!*

Dead Relatives Are the Best Kind — They Don't Come For Visits

Genealogy would be great if it just didn't involve relatives. Now don't get me wrong, I'm all for relatives, especially at a distance, or those who can safely be classed as being circa pre-1850. But most of us have just about as much as we can handle on such festive occasions as Christmas and Thanksgiving, putting up with the irritating souls who happen to be related to us and who live close by, to last us all year long without deliberately going out and hunting for additional ones. Those of you who are not afflicted with genealogy as a hobby probably assume that we who are suffer from some kind of warped psychological and uncontrollable need to surround ourselves with family members. Well, mostly we do, but on 3 x 5 cards. An ideal relative, as far as we are concerned, is no more than a neatly typed, correctly spelled full name on a regulation-size family group sheet. We'd happily wallow about in huge numbers of those. You see, the typed name can't start a family squabble by making a pass at your wife or husband. The typed name can't upstage you by being richer, handsomer, fancier dressed or a better conversationalist. If he or she has taken prizes for selling insurance, doing weird things with rocks, or dancing a hot tango, you don't have to sit still while they recount the boring details or perform a sample of their terpsichorean prowess in person. (If they tell you all about it in a letter, you can always skip that part.) Accordingly, unless their letters are so totally abrasive as to cause constant offense, you will most likely continue on friendly writing terms with the distant kin for the very reason that they *are* distant and stay that way.

But supposing the day comes when you detect that one of them (or more than one, if you're really unlucky) begins to show the dreaded signs, in his or her letters, of the telltale, not-too-subtle hints that they might actually be contemplating a VISIT. Should you panic! *YOU BET!* Then, once you have toned down your hysteria, you had better immediately start mapping out strategy for squelching their fiendish desires right square in the bud (i.e. before they load their suitcases in their car and leave home, headed in your direction). First of all, you might consider firing off a plausible reason for why you won't be home (the entire remainder of the year, just to be on the safe side) or, if home, why you simply cannot entertain visitors during that particular time, much as you would dearly *love* to, of course. Don't use humdrum, time-worn excuses. Try to be more colorful and inventive. You could regale them with the fascinating news that you have just won a round-trip ticket to Tibet, and you plan to stay there awhile. Or you might claim you have been ordered to check into a nearby hospital (which is out-of-bounds to visitors) so that a series of exotic tests can be run on you to determine what qualities are best avoided in outer space. (You could qualify the tests as physical ones if you wanted to maintain postal contact with this particular set of relatives at a later date, and mental ones if you did not.) Or you might wish to embark on an entirely different tack by penning a bubbly, upbeat, cooperative letter, saying that you are eagerly awaiting their visit, assuring them that you have plenty of room to put them up and simply would not hear of their staying in a motel. Then, ever so casually, slip in what you pray will be the clincher, that you have just recently opened your home as a much-needed convalescent center for live-in AIDS patients, but that you know they (your dear relatives) will be sympathetic because these unfortunate boarders are all very friendly and have been a big help to you in preparing all the family meals and making sure the paroled rapist living in the back bedroom doesn't get out of hand too often. That should pretty well turn potential guests unpotential.

But suppose the genealogical pen-pals on your family

tree never give you the chance to take such evasive action in advance but decide, on the spur of the moment, to leave for your house, perhaps informing you of the fact by recording a message on your answering machine or dropping you a last-minute letter as they leave home base which reaches you one day prior to their intended arrival. You may not have sufficient time to order a "QUARANTINED" sign professionally printed. You could always leave town on the day in question, but it would be just your luck to have their camper parked in your driveway waiting for you when you returned, especially if they have inherited the strong family trait of stubborn perseverance. You could, of course, resort to the standard escape scenario whereby you park your car down the block, tightly close all your drapes and hide in your house, being careful not to make even the faintest noise, until they go away (a ploy you have practiced successfully a few times when you've gotten word that your pesty brother-in-law was coming over to borrow money). But this trick would be difficult at best if you were not sure of the exact day or time of day they were due to arrive. It might also prove embarrassing if the hastily-tied gag on your indoor dog slipped off and he started barking or if a smart-aleck neighbor kid figured out what you were doing and blew the whistle on you by so informing all callers. Unfortunately, fellow genealogyphiles, the sad truth is that visits from relatives can best be compared to an invasion of fruit flies—you probably won't be able to stop them!

Unless the expected visitors have sent pictures of themselves ahead of time, they are never going to look like what you imagine they should look like. If you took genetics in college and got an "A" in it, you might understand what I'm talking about and not be overly surprised. Otherwise it's best to keep a blank mind. As is the case with most genealogists, all the time you have been patiently typing stacks and stacks of family group sheets, you could see each person, in your mind's eye, as another clone of the members of your own family branch—short, dumpy, blue-eyed, high-foreheaded, funny-nosed creatures. So then how does one react when a six-foot four-inch beanpole with close-set, beady little brown eyes shows up? On closer inspection, you would swear he has had a nose job or else got awfully lucky when it came to that part of his anatomy. But then, in the forehead department, you can definitely feel superior, because his sort of looks like an ape's, in fact, and doesn't do justice to the family at all. And how in blue blazes does he manage to stay so slim when you know you can't even have a harmless little chocolate sundae now and then without looking like a walking version of the Goodyear blimp? Sure beats all how you could have both come out of the same blooming ancestor!

You know, I had hoped I would be able to skim through this particular discussion without getting into the thoroughly dull subject of genetics, but I suppose one can't avoid it. Frankly, it is extremely difficult to introduce such a learned topic, the complexities of which will be above the heads of most of you. I hesitate to admit it, being somewhat modest, but it isn't true that I was at the top of my class in genetics. In fact, I didn't even take it, choosing instead the more grueling and scholarly elective of Leather Work (straight, of course, not kinky, even though it was taught here in California). Since it is common knowledge that you can place the blame for any deviant looking person in your family right smack on genetics, I tried to find a genitalist, or whatever they call themselves, to explain it to you, but they were all busy experimenting and wouldn't cooperate. So it looks like the burden will fall on me to prepare an erudite, scientific explanation for why you shouldn't be too shocked to discover that some of your family members look different than others (just so it isn't *too* different, you understand).

You start out this whole business back somewhere in the Dark Ages with one pure ancestor (don't ask me where *he* came from, that part gets too technical), but since the guy was an ancestor, that meant he had the duty to marry someone. In those days, to be effective, it was required the person be a female and this usually meant bringing into the family an Outsider with strange genes and cells and things, thereby polluting up the Purity no end till eventually, after a few generations of this sort of behavior, no one looked like anyone else anymore. Are you still following this rather complicated dissertation? Now, if your ancestor married his first-cousin, however, he wouldn't dilute everything up so bad and their issue (you'll notice I'm not referring to them as kids) would inherit all the good stuff double. If only each male descendant had married only his first-cousin, we could pretty well predict what the issue would turn out like. In fact, it would be much the same as dogs registered with the A.K.C. But I guess it was better that they ran amok and mongrelized everything because we couldn't have afforded building mental institutions to house almost everyone. That is about all I can spare you right now in the way of a genetic lecture.

What kind of excitement can you offer the distant relative who is also a genealogy freak? When they come to visit me out here in California, I know they haven't driven across all that desolation just to see the Golden Gate Bridge, nude beaches, or the redwoods. No, it's my file cabinets that are the scenic attractions, I'm sure of it! If they only plan to stay one day, I sit them right down on a

straight-backed chair at the dining room table and plop a pile of Xeroxed land records in front of them so that they can peruse in gay abandon. I make it a point never to serve liquid refreshment to any of these visitors for a number of very good reasons. One is that I have never mastered the intricate art of making coffee and, besides, I've heard coffee runs right through someone who has been traveling. Our facilities, unfortunately, don't cotton to being overloaded, being at the mercy of a temperamental septic tank as we are, and quite often our water system isn't operating at all. Needless to say, we do not encourage much flushing. Another reason, almost too embarrassing to confess, is that there is a strain of tragic individuals in our family who have gone down that misguided path toward total temperance. If I were to offer *them* something (if you will pardon the expression) alcoholic, I'm sure they would lapse into icy *hauteur* and I would wind up the captive recipient of a two-hour lecture on abstinence.

The choice of food causes almost as many problems. If you offer a plate containing squid, tofu, sliced jicama, and an artichoke to an average person from Kansas, they simply become unglued. On the other hand, a Berkeley visitor to the farm belt probably wouldn't know how to "interact his lifestyle" with beef, mashed potatoes and gravy. I knew I had made some kind of epicurean *faux pas*, for instance, when a visiting coal miner from Illinois informed me, after a perfectly ordinary meal at our table, that his mother had always told him to eat everything that was put before him, even if he couldn't figure out what it was. (It still remains a puzzle to me why he suddenly felt the need to share that old homily with us at that particular time.)

Once you have exhausted the sharing of food, liquid refreshment (of whatever type and quantity you dare), and bundles of ancestral records with your visiting kin, and they are still sitting there in your house expectantly, what can possibly be left to amuse them? A delightful couple back in Kentucky, who happened to be my kinfolk, came up with an entertaining idea when our regular conversation petered out to nearly a standstill as we were visiting them. (Yes, curious readers, I confess, I am as guilty as the next person of the crime of paying visits to relatives.) Anyway, those dear Kentuckians, who were quite elderly and more than a little infirm, loaded us in their huge old car and announced that they were taking us to the family cemetery. With that, we went careening off down the road, staying square astraddle of the white line which, we gathered, was one thing the driver could still see reasonably well most of the time. Luckily, while fleeting glimpses of the faces of the drivers we met confirmed the fact that most of them bore terrified expressions, they all managed to swerve out of our way, so that there were no casualties. Of course it was safer when we weren't driving on the regular roads at all but just extemporaneously meandering off across the countryside, waving at startled tobacco farmers tending their crops, and trying to avoid too much entanglement with such annoying obstacles as brier patches and trees. On the way back from the very precious and private time spent at the final resting place of so many family members, our improvised guided tour took us up and down a number of "hollows" of special family importance. The running commentary consisted mainly of pointing out the spots where various kin had lived, taken a bullet, raised crops, fell out of their cars, or otherwise been party to a significant happening. With the passage of time, other sightseeing trips may become blurred and forgotten, but not that one. The lesson here is that you can always invent something to do with infernal visiting relatives that will remain, for them at least, a lasting impression.

Before we leave the subject of sightseeing, one additional controversial thought should be brought to your attention. That is. how do you determine whether the soon-to-be guests are proposing a trip to your house because of a genuine and consuming interest in *you,* as a person, or merely to get a look at your scenic wonders? It can be quite a blow to your self-esteem if they drive clear out from Little Rock and, after five minutes of sparkling conversation with you, ask the way to the Hearst Castle. Of course, those of you who live in boring parts of the country that can barely come up with enough "Recreational and Historical Sites" to fill the required space on your local road map (like Iowa, for instance) can rest assured *your* visitors, if you ever have any, have sought you out because of your winning personality displayed in your letters or the fact that you are the possessor of the family Bible or some other legitimate reason and not just because you live next door to Gettysburg or Yellowstone Park or some other such tourist attraction. If you are conveniently located within a short distance of a whole lot of these Points of Interest, you are in big trouble and may never see a relative-free summer again. But that is what we risk by messing around with such a hobby in the first place!

By the way, I hope the dear souls who have already visited us or those who may, even as I am writing this, be laying plans for an upcoming trip, should they somehow get a look at this book, will know that I didn't mean *them* in this part of it. In fact, figuring that this section might offend, insult or otherwise cause mental anguish to possible future visitors, not to mention those who have already completed the act, made me seriously hesitate before I even included such a section at all, strongly debating with myself that very possibility for all of five seconds before going ahead with it (heh, heh, heh).

Once you have alienated all your visitors, past, present and future, used up your allotment of postage stamps, collected your last snotty reply from a County Clerk, and run smack-dab into a brick wall as far as any further genealogical progress is concerned, you have every right to ask yourself a momentous question: "What in the dickens do I do now with all this junk?" Well, who amongst us has not at some time in his or her life felt the burning desire to see his or her name on the spine and cover of a book? And you've said to yourself that many of the books written nowadays appear to have been done by idiots, morons and other unbalanced folks so, by golly, you probably have as much chance as the next one to become an author.

Writing the Book
the Whole World
is Waiting For

Bringing up the subject of publishers first in this chapter may be compared by some of you to putting the rear end of a horse before the head end. (Not that there is any deliberate intention here, mind you, of equating a publisher with that particular part of the equine anatomy, perish the thought!) Come to think of it, perhaps it is not too wise to poke fun at publishers at all. There really isn't an overabundance of wild humor about them anyhow and if you are foolish enough to take them on in a book that is yet to be published (by them), they might spell your name wrong or print some of the pages upside-down in retaliation. But, here goes. . . .

If you are smart, like me, of course, and choose the absolutely *BEST* publisher, you shouldn't suffer any major disasters, so long as you can come up with the payments. But if you comparison shop all over the place in an attempt to ferret out the cheapest bargain price and then decide to take your chances with an outfit that just set up shop last week with a borrowed printing press, you might be kicking yourself right in your file cabinet before you are through. I have heard horror stories from other authors that would spin your projector-crank!

Supposing your family surname is POWSHIEWESK-SICZ and, as stands to reason, you plan to use it as part of your title. Well, you can bet they will mess it up somehow. If they promise your book will be done by December, you had better ask what year. If they quote you a "Publishing Price," but the little bitty print says that there may be a few separate, extra charges (e.g. telephone calls, postage, paper, binding, containers, mailing, handling, miscellaneous, etc.), it might not be such a bad idea to go right out and select a lawyer you won't mind spending a lot of time with because, chances are, you are going to need one. If the glorious day you have always dreamed about finally arrives and all your messy scribbling is miraculously transformed into a printed reality, proudly displayed in your home, only to have the color on the cover turn your antique coffee table and your equally antique Aunt Agnes' hands bright crimson and, even worse, the pages fall out about the third time you open it, it might dawn on you that you chose the wrong publisher.

Now, as for the human beings who collect their paychecks from the firms who publish individual family histories—they must be masochists, at the very least, to go on working for this type of megalomaniac press. Consequently, I would imagine that the more far-seeing among them, to keep from becoming total basket cases, would eventually turn in their walking papers and hightail it to the nearest pornographic house, seeking alternate and much more stomachable employment. Those timid souls who remain behind probably keep commiserating with themselves that if only they were affiliated with the hoity-toity commercial houses instead, they would enjoy the

power and satisfaction of being able to send out rejection slips to about 99½ % of what they are now forced to accept at their present place of business. Unfortunately, since their house motto is "Anything Goes" (so long as it is accompanied by a check), they wearily resign themselves to gritting their teeth and wading through the sludge. It must be especially trying for those brilliant individuals who were English majors in college, unless they are drunk or on something all the time. But, before we become too sympathetic toward their plight, let's face it, in reality and as much as we would like to believe otherwise, I doubt that you would ever catch them actually *proof-reading* anything. No, I suspect that "proof-reading", in their own special vernacular, merely means counting the pages as quickly as possible and not paying any attention to the typewritten bilge they contain. Mathematical skills must be considered of the highest priority in their job specs because, without counting, how would the publishing house know that the fee they plan to charge is as high as it could possibly be. Employees at the prestigious, five-star firms, putting out these same kind of books, must devote long hours shaping their counting skills to a finely honed perfection, because not only will they be expected to arrive at an accurate total, but they will also have to handle the vastly more complicated assignment of deducing whether the little numbers at the top or bottom of the pages have been placed there correctly in a reasonable attempt at standardly recognized chronological order. That is pretty heady responsibility! You can hardly expect them to do anything about the places in your finished product where you dropped your Hershey bar on the typewriter keyboard and it made a lot of funny little marks, or where your dog's paw playfully hit the keys right in the middle of some of your best narrative. Their union contract probably protects them from actually having to read any of your stuff anyway.

When there is a reference in your bill to "handling," I would guess that is synonymous with the attempt to heft whatever weird objects the postman off-loads in the lobby of the publishing house (if it is a large enough publishing house to have a lobby). I've been told that the typical incoming manuscript (and they must use this term with a great deal of barely controlled hysterical laughter) which is sent to them can arrive in anything from a solid steel crate to a bedraggled shoe-box precariously held together by masking tape. In most cases, I'm sure, the crate has a greater monetary value than the enclosed manuscript. Shucks, the shoe-box probably has a greater monetary value, but one doesn't tell the client that.

If the publisher's representative (do they refer to themselves as editors, if they don't edit anything?) has been doing a thorough pre-publication job, he or she has convinced the author-to-be to lay out money for a ream or more of regulation publisher's masters on which to do their own bloody typing. But avoiding this aggravating chore doesn't necessarily guarantee that all will be smooth sailing for the publishing house employee who, every so often, is saddled with the unpleasant duty of informing the cooperative but not too bright sender-turned-typist that he or she has just typed 1517, or whatever, pages all wrong. The problem here, as we see it, is not with the typist, however, but with the picky publisher who is not very understanding, nor sympathetic, about standard genealogical operating procedures. Most of us genealogists, not being terribly wealthy, have become indoctrinated over the years with a frugality that does not recognize such silly extravagances as margins. Therefore, they can hardly expect us to notice, or even understand the reason for, all those pretty blue lines on the publishing masters. All we know is that if we are paying by the page to have our family immortalized in print, by crickety, we intend to get our money's worth by not wasting space. The difficult job of re-education falls squarely on the publisher who, if he is both wise and diplomatic, will stress the fact that both Ernest HEMINGWAY and Edna FERBER didn't put out books with the writing running right off the page. Patience and flattery work wonders, I'm told, and are probably the only tools to use against a reluctant genealogist-author with a history of bad habits and a stubborn disposition.

Occasionally, family historians choose not to do their own typing, either because of laziness or lack of a typewriter, or because they are big spenders who have better things to do with their time. Consequently, they can cause even more massive headaches than the margin-ignorers, above. Rarely are their submissions anything less than abominable. It must take a dedicated and patient publisher's employee with exceptional eyesight indeed to deal with 900 or so pages of onion skin paper, completely covered on both sides with nearly undecipherable handwriting all done with that kind of pencil that comes off on your hands. So I suppose we must grudgingly give them their due, no matter what kind of an outlandish publishing fee they come up with. I guess their work ought to be worth at least something.

Before we leave the fascinating subject of self-publishing, there is a need to cover one more aspect of it, the scariest one of all for budding first-time authors who are soon to blossom forth into do-it-yourself book marketeers. Just how many copies do you dare order? Oh, you say smugly, that will be no problem for you because you plan to pre-sell your book well before the publishing time, so you are sure you will know exactly. Oh yeah! Where do you think you are going to come up with the selling price, from a crystal ball? Most semi-intelligent folk (the type who would be most likely to buy your book) won't purchase a book unless they know what it costs. You won't know what to charge per copy until you tell your publisher how many books you want. Get the picture? And if you think I am going to tell you the magic formula for figuring this out, you have another think coming. I had enough trouble with this myself, so it's every man for himself (or woman, if that's your persuasion). I can tell you, however, that there are certain basic rules of ordering. The more you order the less you pay each. The less you order the more chance you have of running out, except that you will have to charge more, so you might sell less. The more you order the more you will probably sell because you will charge less but pay more. Are you having trouble following this? So am I. Unfortunately, the same clear rules hold true for trying to establish the fairest price to charge per copy, once you have some idea what it is going to cost you. Does one charge the lowest price possible to just barely cover the cost, thereby guaranteeing a loss because of the complimentary copies you will have to disburse, but probably selling more books in the long run? Or does one throw decency to the winds and gouge the buyers unmercifully for all one can get? You had best pick a day when you have a really clear head to figure out all these important matters.

Now that we have covered the last subject first, we will move backwards to the first subject last. (I can't help it if you don't have a good grasp of logic and fail to understand simple progression, or is it that rather complicated discussion, above, which has gotten you all mixed up?) Anyhow, now that we have talked about publishing the book, we had best cover how you are ever going to manage to write the varmint in the first place. It takes more than just putting a blank piece of paper in your trusty typewriter and trying to harness whatever faculties you may still possess in order to make a maximum effort at thinking. That old paper can stay blank a good long time, let me tell you, unless you have Formulated a Plan, Become Organized, or Drawn a Diagram (as every good "how-to" book worth its price will keep yammering at you to do).

That first sheet of paper won't look nearly as blank if you start typing (or writing) section or chapter headings or possible choice for a title on it (or SOMETHING, for goodness sake, instead of just sitting there like a zombie!). Sure, it may take you months to progress beyond that point (some *never* do), but you can at least claim that you are now "writing" if some curious member of your household asks you why you are spending so much time sitting at the kitchen table looking stupified. And, boy, can you ever use it to make a big impression on folks, by saying, "No, Edna, I can't go to the rummage sale. I have my writing, you know." At the same time you dramatically put your hand to your forehead and sigh with fervor. If Edna doesn't assume you have just been hitting the muscatel, she might become suitably impressed. And there is no limit as to places where you can bring up the subject. A glowing account to the bagger at the supermarket checkout counter will clue him in to the fact that he is serving a celebrity and he might not put those heavy gallon cans right square on top of that $3.98 basket of strawberries next time. So don't hesitate to flail the information about hither and yon, wherever it will do the most good.

At some point in time, however, you will have to get beyond the point of jotting down possible titles and chapter headings. This is called The Turning Point. You either give up being a writer or you actually write something. It's as simple as that!

Since a family history had better be about a family, that simplifies the outline of it right there. You do have some choices, you realize, about how in the world you are going to do it. The worst possible example is the book which appears to be nothing but one meandering, totally confused family chart, using a formula of numbering you have never seen before (and never will again, I'll wager), no sources because that takes up too much room, and no index, for the very same reason. At the other extreme are the fancy, enjoyable genealogies liberally sprinkled with pictures of grim, forbidding people sitting or standing in extremely uncomfortable poses and doing a pretty good job of looking like ancestors should. Young readers, catching sight of these pictures, will burst out laughing and declare that they are glad they didn't live in the olden days (even when talking about your own pictures taken in the 1940s, fool kids!). For an added benefit, you can always use the pictures to threaten your own offspring

that, if they don't do as they are told, the meanest looking ancestor will come back in the middle of the night and haunt them. Granted, this may cause nightmares, but the little shavers will at least know what their forebears looked like.

One of the most ticklish items which will confront the family historian involves the controversial subject of censorship. In plain English, do you expose yourself to the whole world by Letting It All Hang Out? Or do you take it upon yourself to sanitize the family chronicles completely by turning all those records you disapprove of into a gigantic bonfire, *à la* Adolph HITLER? It depends, I guess, on whether you want Posterity to read your book and become instantly Aghast! Then, too, there is the monetary aspect. If Great Aunt Jane made her living on the streets, her descendants might willingly subsidize your whole literary endeavor in an attempt to keep that fact under wraps. Notwithstanding, I subscribe to the school of thought that since most genealogies are deadly dull, why not spice them up a bit by leaving in the attempted and/or successful poisonings, the colorful bigamists, gay or otherwise, the merry little tales of how your family came to acquire the very best horseflesh in the entire county without benefit of a bill of sale, the wife-beating and other deviant hobbies practiced when they could think of no better way of occupying their time. If you do this, you should sell books like mad, if for no other reason than to keep them from getting out on the market.

So, go to it, my fellow genealogists, and write that book, dull or scandalous. Otherwise, that 30 years' worth of diligent research might go up in a matter of seconds if those scatterbrained heirs of yours, who can barely read, get their grubby hands on it. (There, that should leave you with something to worry about!)

Before you toss this little masterpiece in with yesterday's fish bones, coffee grounds and other such goodies designed for the incinerator, you might want to check out the Officially Approved Words in the back of this book. If you aren't educated enough by now, that may do it!

Appropriate Words to Fling About

Note: I don't like the word "Glossary." It's like "circa," too phony. "Glossary" sounds like something you'd smear on furniture. But if it makes those of you who are high-brows and sticklers for tradition feel more secure to keep everything downright technical, then you can go ahead and call this section by that silly name.

For the uninitiated (including all you poor miserable beginners), the following is a list of words which are thrown around daily by us old-timers in the genealogy field. You will give less of an impression of being a dunce if you memorize the terms and their meanings. The pronunciations are not included because you shouldn't say most of these words out loud anyway.

Abstract—In this case we are not referring, as you may have thought, to the percentage of genealogists who are obviously suffering from the advanced stage of "abstraction," which is mental withdrawal and absent-mindedness. Now, where were we again? Oh, yes. The "abstract" used here is something you can blame a conniving lawyer or county clerk, or both, on. You can mostly find them (the abstracts, that is, not the lawyer and county clerk, unless they have something going) in the vaults of the courthouse.

Ancestor—A person who gave so little thought to how important he would be to someone someday that he didn't commit nearly enough significant acts to get himself noticed, at least not in counties with fireproof courthouses. Instead of performing stupendous, momentous deeds to guarantee a place in the county history books, he just frit-

tered away his time doing dumb things like pulling up trees or chopping them down, plodding along behind a mule and plow, keeping his wife (or wives) pregnant, or getting punctured by arrows. If he were alive today, you wouldn't even invite him to a party.

Branch—This word was almost surely added to the genealogists' vocabulary by the same tree-fetishist who started the whole silly habit of calling ancestral charts family trees. Within some families certain descriptive words are used to further identify descendants of this person or that one, such as: the strange branch, the snooty branch, the criminal branch, the branch we don't talk about, etc. The funny thing about this word is that even if you are cut off completely, you remain as firmly joined as ever to your branch, which remains forever attached to your tree, severed or not. Tell that one to the next arborist you meet.

Census—Stuff government employees pried out of our ancestors, when they weren't busy fighting bloodthirsty Indians or inventing things to make themselves more modern. Said information, if it isn't unreadable, outright lies, or junk made up by a lazy or frightened census-taker who didn't want to ride clear out to your family's farm because of an ongoing feud, or the vicious dogs to be found there, might be of possible value to you. Some of it burned up so won't be of much help.

Circa—If you see this word, or just a "ca" alongside something, what it means is "about" and I will never understand why they don't simply say "about." It must have been started by those same snobbish college professors who refer to janitors as sanitary engineers. Why, just think how foolish it would sound if I said, "I'm *circa* to go crazy!" I, for one, am not *about* to ever use this word!

Circuit Court, Clerk of the—Since circuit means the act of going around something, don't ever expect to pin these folks down long enough in one spot to find your records. Clerk, on the other hand, means priest, so someone certainly messed up somewhere and maybe that's what we should put in those county offices. At least they would treat you with more sympathy and not take such long lunch hours as those cranky imposters who are so firmly entrenched at the present time.

Clan—This means offshoot and that is exactly what mine were doing, mostly, off shooting at other clans.

Coat-of-Arms (also see Crest)—An inspirational drawing, usually featuring lions or eagles, that separates the upper-crust from the unwashed peasants. If you want to spend your money to prove you are better than average, you can have one made up to tack on your garage door or to put on a shield (if you live in California and perchance carry one). If your stationery has been imprinted with it too, people will just naturally treat you with more reverence. Even bill collectors may call you "Sir."

Compile—What you do if you can't write stuff on your own. Since I am a compiler in my own right, due to that big, thick family history, I took instant offense to the definition of this word in my dictionary. It said "plunder"! That is too close to "steal" and I resent it! Even though those of us who engage in this practice copy down things we find elsewhere, we don't take kindly to being accused of it.

Computer—A modern and wondrously labor-saving invention which, when installed at the check-out counter of a store, will guarantee that it will take you five times as long to conduct business as in the olden days when the

clerk merely announced the price out loud and you paid it. Of course, whatever human is in charge of the annoying thing always comes up with such excuses as, "The computer is down" or "The hard disc has ossified" or "The floppy disc has flipped someplace and we can't find it." The tragic truth is that this silly, here-today-gone-tomorrow gadget has now invaded our sacred halls of genealogy, so be on your guard!

Crest—We are not talking about growths on the heads of chickens here, but something you put on wineglasses, plaques, and the pockets of your blazer to prove your ancestors stood for something! I get this mixed up with Coat-of-Arms, above, but I think you put the two of them together somehow to impress others who don't have one.

Descendant—Your own dear children and loving grandchildren, but you wish they wouldn't make so much noise, interrupt, or bother you when you are trying to pay attention to relatives who have had the decency to be long since departed. What do the little toads think family history involves, anyhow?

Descent—A very depressing word indeed for the gene-alogist who spends his whole life striving to be on top of the heap, because it means downward. That puts those of us who are around nowadays at the very *bottom* (or not much further than a couple of steps up, if we already have children and grandchildren). And, no matter how hard you work at it, there is very little hope for much upward movement until after you are a long time dead and prob-ably won't care anymore. For the overly ambitious climber, this word is a downer.

Exogamy—I put this one in here for you superior intellectuals who have not taken up the filthy practice of cross-pollination. Did you know that it is often inviolable and that means you had better keep on doing it or you might start producing crazies.

Family Chart—A sheet someone took a lot of time designing, which shows your pedigree, like a dog's when applying to the American Kennel Club for registration. The more spaces you are able to fill in, the more uppity you can act around people with only two or three names on theirs.

File Cabinet—What you buy when your spouse says, "You have 24 hours to get all this junk off the dining room table!" Once you have one, however, it will give you lots more room in which to store all those important death certificates, land records and stuff no one will ever look at again. Unfortunately, it will probably be the first item your spouse or heirs chuck out once you have "Gone to Your Reward."

Genealogist—What you tell your husband or wife you are when he or she asks why you want to keep going out nights to go to the library. If the response is, "Oh, YEAH!", you had better be able to prove it. A *real* one is a person with a mind in the past (or is it *on* the past?), a briefcase full of undecipherable notes, and health problems from sitting down too much. It isn't "sissy" to be one, by the way, because men descended from something too, and may be curious as to what.

Genealogy — Sometimes confused with "geology," where you also dig up stuff. But with genealogy it's expired relatives, not rocks. It took me four years to even spell it right.

Heraldry—I think this has something to do with an unmentionable function performed by a pervert named Herald who is desperately trying to keep himself covered by his armorial bearings. We had better not get too far into this questionable subject in a family-oriented book.

Heredity—If you have a gene in your chromosome and it gets stuck in your transmission and causes problems, you can blame the whole mess on some ancestor who lived in the olden days and should have known better. I think this refers more to passing down instead of passing out, but if your branch wasn't 100% temperance, it could mean either. Actually, you have no control at all of it before it descends on you and, considering the scandalous way the younger generation behaves these days, probably not much more control after yours has petered out.

Index—Something in the back of the book you look for first and utter loud and blasphemous phrases if you don't find one. Of such value as to be sometimes printed and sold separately to name freaks, those eccentric individuals whose idea of the ultimate in entertainment is to sit by the hour and read endless lists of names.

Inferior Court—A term which used to be used to distinguish this particular legal entity from the Superior one. Nowadays, since it is so widely recognized that they are all that way, and we can't do much about it, wasting one's breath on this term is no longer necessary.

Intestate—The mistaken notion that you could beat the system if you didn't write a will. Others who wound up this way were those who died when they had no intention of doing so, mostly of lead poisoning brought on by bullets, and those who were so miserly as to believe they would be allowed to take it with them.

Microfiche—Contrary to what you may think, these are not little bitty cold-blooded vertebrate animals, unless that is what you think your ancestors were and someone took a polaroid picture of them with a very small camera. If you beginners want to pose as blasé, just saunter into the research center with your briefcase at a rakish angle and drop this word a few times (e.g. "Do you have pastel microfiche?" or "I'll show you my microfiche, baby, if you'll show me yours" or "Who in the microfiche stole my family chart?"). Then you won't stand out.

Military Records—Obtained from Washington, D.C., national seat of red tape, foul-ups and money extraction. Pieces of paper confirming the fact that your ancestor refused to fight in the Revolutionary War and was then arrested, or had a bad case of the trots in the Civil War and had to be discharged, or was in the vicinity of an official battle somewhere. All that is left from our first glorious conflict, the Revolutionary War, is what those heathen limeys couldn't find and set fire to.

Pedigree—This actually is a crane's foot, so it seems like a pretty peculiar term for genealogists to be bandying about, but darned if they don't do it anyway. Maybe it got started because a bunch of researchers standing around in the library stacks with their necks stretched out, searching for especially juicy items, bore such a striking resemblance to a gaggle of cranes standing in a swamp, that it was unavoidable. On the other hand, if the crane referred to was the mechanical version that is always lifting a lot of big heavy objects, then it might have originated with the genealogist who constantly totes around overloaded briefcases (see page 4). How the "foot" part got in there is another mystery, but I'm sure your ancestor probably had one, if not two.

Projector—A complicated piece of equipment you will just have to learn to master or you will never get off the genealogical launch-pad. They come in two kinds: automatic pilot for those with chronic bursitis and an "A" in speed-reading, and manual for the dim-witted, sluggish, and those of us who don't trust new-fangled gadgets and like to be in control at all times. There are a variety of models, all equipped with funny little mechanical protuberances of all sorts, most of which are not working. The most important of these are the crank, the light switch (which might actually be extremely complicated, if it has "high" and "low"), and the thingamajig that lets you correct the focus (unless you are used to being out of focus and prefer it that way).

Public—Always be sure to include the "L" in this word, or you may be the target of some very shocked glances in your direction. Used properly, this word means that which county employees try to keep as far away as possible from records of the same name. "Open to the knowledge of all," for some totally unfathomable reason, is freely translated in certain courthouses to "KEEP OUT!" The public, and you as a visible representative of it, may be a very nasty word indeed in some of these government bastions, so best be prepared for fisticuffs at a moment's notice when trying to get your hands on what is rightfully yours.

Research — The act of impersonating Sherlock HOLMES and digging up all the dirt you can find on your family.

Roots—Another example which points to the fact that whoever drew up the Marquess of Queensberry rules for this hobby had an unhealthy perversion regarding trees, but it's too late to change it now. If someone comes up to you in a genealogy society meeting and tries to coax you into displaying yours, there is no need to belt the individual (unless the invitation is extended outside in the dark parking lot after the meeting has adjourned). One thing this word has going for it is that most roots (correct me if I'm wrong) are down in the ground. Since most ancestors are, too, maybe it's apropos?

Vital Records—I'll bet your ancestor would have never dreamed that when he dropped down dead of the ague, his passing would be so critical (except to himself and his immediate dependents), of such crucial importance and so indispensable to the whole civilized world of genealogy as to be actually published in a book, the title of which usually incorporates use of this term in all its hysterical meaning.

Zygote—No matter what you may have listed on your family chart as your first ancestor, this is what you came from (I wouldn't kid you, look it up).